From Strategy t

Develop a winning organisational strategy and convert it into success

From Strategy to Success

Develop a winning organisational strategy and convert it into success

Anthony J Wilkinson

First edition - 2019

Pen-2-Paper

www.pen-2-paper.co.uk

Pen-2-Paper

86-90 Paul Street, London, EC2A 4NE

www.pen-2-paper.co.uk

ISBN: 9781083169211

First Edition Published 2019

Copyright © Pen-2-Paper, 2019. All rights reserved.

The moral right of the author has been asserted.

No part of this publication may be reproduced, distributed or transmitted in any form or by any means, including printing, photocopying or other electronic or mechanical methods, without the prior written consent of the publisher, except as permitted under Copyright Law.

About the Author

Throughout his working life, Anthony Wilkinson has been involved in organisational development across many industries. He has a natural flair for improvement and an instinct to identify where effective changes would be beneficial; Anthony has successfully transformed many leading organisations.

As a spotty teenager, Anthony wanted to be a design engineer. Through his determination, the dream eventually became a reality but, as a newly qualified draughtsman, Anthony realised he wanted more from life. After a further spell in fulltime education, he embarked upon a successful career in corporate development.

In his book, From Strategy to Success, Anthony shares his knowledge and experience of developing winning strategies and translating them into success by effectively managing organisational change.

The strategic planning process begins with a statement of the objective and ends with the achievement of the objective.

Anthony J Wilkinson, 2019

Preface: Change is inevitable

Whatever an organisation does, and regardless of its past performance, change is unavoidable.

Organisations continuously face pressures and influences, forcing them to change. Launching new products and services, improving processes and productivity, or expanding into untapped markets, all require significant change. Emerging technologies, increased competition, new regulations, and evolving customer trends, force organisations to do things differently.

Any planned change must result in improvement; organisations should aim to change for the better. However, it's not always the case. When organisations talk about change and the management of change, they refer to planned change, which will lead to growth or survival.

For the change to result in success, the organisation must determine where they are now, where they want to be, and how they're going to get there. Using a logical approach and considering all influencing factors before they become problems, organisations can change, improve and grow.

This book describes how to develop a winning strategy, devise plans for its implementation, and effectively manage organisational change.

Acknowledgements

I believe I've learnt something from everyone I've ever worked with; so, even though I can't remember all the names, I thank you!

Credits

All photographs and illustrations © Caroline Lin.

Photograph One: Change

Dedications

I dedicate this book to my parents, my brother, and my sister; each motivates and supports me in a special way.

Thank you.

List of figures, tables, illustrations and photographs

Figures One: Hierarchy structure 3
Two: Organisational structure 4
Three: Performance trend 9
Four: Example of a Project Plan 17
Five: Plans and activities 22
Six: Communication structure 26
Seven: Cascading structure 35

Tables One: The crystal ball 88
Two: Tabulated Project Plan 95

Illustrations One: Building a pyramid 2
Two: FMEA chart 63

Photographs One: Change iii
Two: On your marks 1
Three: This book is aimed at YOU 11
Four: Bad meeting 60
Five: Thank you! 67

How to use this book

From Strategy to Success guides the reader through the process of creating an organisational strategy and converting it into action and success, through communication and the involvement of everyone in the organisation.

The book provides a logical step-by-step approach to strategy development, business planning, and cascading those plans through the organisation to every individual. Throughout the content, there is a clear focus on the development of the strategy and its subsequent translation into a business plan.

By offering easy-to-follow guidance at every step, the book shows how the plan develops into success,

I've divided the content into four sections; each part builds upon the previous lessons learnt. While there may appear to be some duplication of one piece to the next, the knowledge gained in each new section builds on the earlier content.

The book starts by setting the scene in Section One and understanding how "change" works.

Here I introduce the concept of the cascade linking the strategy to the tasks.

Inevitably we move on to planning in Section Two; without a detailed Business Plan, the organisation will not identify or implement the required changes.

In Section Three, we look at the tools and controls required to manage the organisation during the period of change.

Finally, in Section Four, we use practical examples to put the knowledge into practice and begin to make the changes.

With clear descriptions and guidance on every aspect of strategy, planning, communicating, and measuring success, the book is intended as a guide and a reference to help the reader define and deliver a winning strategy and a successful organisation.

Throughout the sections I refer to a fictitious organisation – FurnFast – we'll make the introductions shortly. FurnFast is a manufacturer of FURNiture FASTeners. The exercises, case studies and anecdotes show how FurnFast deals (sometimes not very well) with issues around strategy and planning.

Contents

About the author		*i*
Preface: Change is inevitable		*ii*
Acknowledgements and Credits		*iii*
Dedications		*iv*
Lists of figures, tables, illustrations and photographs		*v*
How to use this book		*vi*
Introduction:	**Before we start**	**1**
	What this book is about	2
	The benefits of this methodology	6
	Define the baseline	8
	Is this book for you?	10
	Review	12
Section One	**Setting the scene: All Change!**	**13**
	Change	14
	Market position	14
	Avoid over-reacting	15
	Planning overview	17
	How organisations grow	18
	Measures of success	20
	Being realistic	21
	The costs of failure	21
	Effective management	23
	Before Getting started	26
	Review	28

Section Two	**Planning the changes!**	**29**
	Organisations need a plan	30
	The pitfalls of Business Plans	30
	Business planning	33
	The cascading structure	35
	The plan	36
	Plans can change	37
	Business plan or route plan	38
	Missions and visions	42
	Introducing the Prime Objective	42
	Rules for Business Plans	43
	PESTLE	45
	Introducing FurnFast	47
	Organisation	48
	Review	50
Section Three	**Operational tools and controls**	**51**
	What to expect	52
	Sense of urgency	56
	Revolutionise	56
	Project approval status	58
	Expenditure	58
	Meetings	59
	Recruitment	61
	Tools	61
	Project facilitator	64
	Outside support and expertise	65
	Celebration	66
	Review	68

Section Four	**Making the changes**	**69**
	The baseline	70
	The directors	72
	The Prime Objective	75
	Strategy	79
	The cascading organisation	89
	Management	95
	Formulating the tasks	96
	SMART objectives, targets and tasks	97
	That's it!	98
	Review	99
Annex One	**FurnFast Organisation**	**101**
Annex Two	**FurnFast Products**	**105**
Annex Three	**FurnFast Logistics**	**109**
Annex Four	**FurnFast Manufacturing**	**111**
Annex Five	**FurnFast Operations**	**113**
Glossary		**115**
Index		**121**

Introduction: Before we start

Photograph Two: On your marks

What this book is about

This book is about successfully implementing change in any organisation. The content comes from my experience gleaned from working with many leading organisations across a range of industry sectors. I refrain from telling the reader *what to do*; instead, the book deals with *how to do*. Every organisation is unique; top management must decide *what to do*, using this book to guide them on *how to* develop a winning organisational strategy and convert it into success by managing the required changes.

Organisational structures are often pyramid-shaped with the head at the top and the workers at the bottom. Any attempt to make changes, or to develop the organisation in any way, almost always permeates from top to bottom. In many respects, this is like trying to build a pyramid from the pinnacle downwards; which could be problematic.

For the successful implementation of changes, plans must be developed and effectively communicated from the top; but actions start at the bottom (the foundation) and build upwards. Just like a pyramid.

Illustration One: Building a pyramid

Organisations, like pyramids and other structures, need solid foundations on which to build. In organisations, the workers, not the management, provide those solid foundations.

NOTE: *When I use the term workers, I refer to the people who invariably do the work: driver, nurse, teacher, athlete, trooper, engineer, cleaner, and so on.*

Working with numerous successful organisations over many years, I developed and perfected a process to convert visions into strategies, tasks, and success. This methodology has helped organisations, large and small, achieve unprecedented growth. Irrespective of the industry, this method is beneficial to any organisation that needs, or wants, to change.

The success of this methodology mainly stems from:

- the clearly defined targets,
- the translation and communication of comprehensible messages,
- the roles everyone plays in making change happen, and
- the constant measuring of what is jointly being achieved.

Figure One shows a simple hierarchy structure in the familiar shape of a pyramid. The workers provide a solid foundation, with the supervisors, managers, and so on, above them. With respect, the head of the organisation cannot be the foundation; the head must ask the workers to do that.

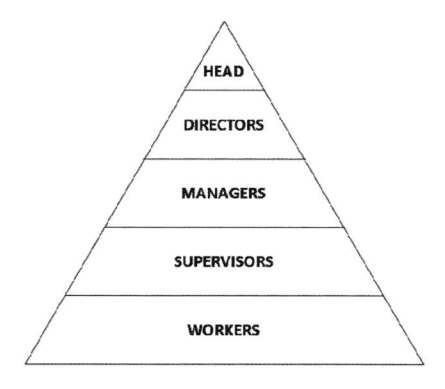

Figure One: Hierarchy structure

Some organisations are keen to get on and make changes, "We don't need a plan"; while others spend too much time putting together Business Plans which, when *published*, remain hidden in drawers and cupboards.

Throughout this book, I recount my experiences of business planning and attempt to highlight the rights and wrongs of managing the change.

Section One starts by setting the scene and understanding how "change" works. I introduce the concept of the cascade linking the strategy to the tasks.

Section Two mainly covers planning; without a detailed plan, the organisation will not identify or implement the required changes.

Section Three introduces the tools and controls required to manage the organisation during the period of change.

Section Four uses practical examples to help the reader put the knowledge into practice and begin to make the changes.

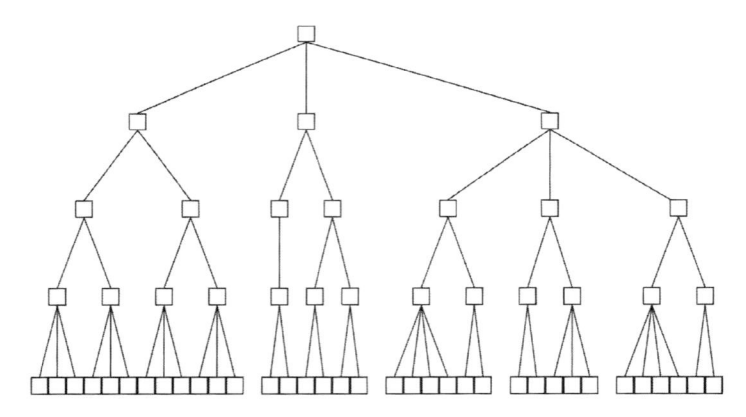

Figure Two: Organisational structure

Figure Two depicts an organisational structure showing the typical distribution of workers, supervisors, managers and directors within the hierarchy.

One critical failing I've observed numerous times is where management impose changes without consideration of the individuals who make the organisation work – the workers. The workers are the foundation of the organisation.

I often ask top management,

"Do you know what Joe Bloggs (a clerk, a machine operative, a driver, a customer service agent, and so on) does?"

Invariably, the directors of an organisation don't usually know what individual workers do.

The two individuals who know precisely what Joe Bloggs does, are Joe Bloggs himself and his supervisor. Likewise, who knows what Joe's supervisor does? The supervisor himself and his manager.

In this type of structure, each worker (on the bottom row) has a link, through their respective supervisor and manager, to the head of the organisation.

Likewise, through the structure, the head is linked to each worker. That is how organisations are constructed; a chain of people connecting the head of the organisation to the workers.

So, when the head announces changes are going to be made, for example, "FurnFast will diversify into complementary markets and products, which should account for over 10% of the new sales revenue", the words have little effect on most of the organisation because the workers don't understand what it means to them, their job, their role and, more importantly, their earnings.

However, why should something the head announces, such as sales revenue, affect Joe Bloggs, who operates a machine all day?

Joe Bloggs doesn't know how the organisation functions; he doesn't understand the significance of the announcement.

The head of the organisation needs to translate his statement and communicate it to the directors in a language they understand. The directors should interpret what they hear and communicate it to the managers, who translate what they hear and deliver it to the supervisors, who go on to explain it to the workers.

At each level, the communicators add detail and ask, "How should we do this?". Through communication and consultation, everyone gets involved in the organisational change.

This is the *Cascading Process*; much more on this later.

Let's go back to Joe Bloggs; what he eventually hears from his supervisor is:

- new products are to be developed to get the organisation into new markets,
- new systems will be designed to automate the process, which will reduce scrap,
- reduced scrap means less waste and, hopefully, more profit,
- working hours will be reviewed to ease fatigue and health issues,
- productivity bonus schemes will be implemented.

What the head said a few weeks ago was "FurnFast will diversify into complementary markets and products, which should account for over 10% of the new sales revenue". With the benefit of the latest information, Joe understands what was said and feels he can play a part in making the changes.

In this example, let's say it took six weeks for the translated and detailed message to get from the head of the organisation to the worker; some people may consider six weeks to be a long time.

However, in my experience, when the head of an organisation makes an important announcement about forthcoming changes, the workers hear nothing but rumours.

The benefits of this methodology

The advantage of using this approach is the achievement of the objective.

This is not an absolute guarantee, but if:

- the organisation is realistic in its expectations,
- the plans are formulated and cascaded,
- the individuals work as a team, and
- the process is understood and followed,

the organisation can expect to achieve what it plans to do.

From my experience, organisations can also expect additional 'spin-off' benefits, such as:

Planning and scheduling improvements; anticipated improvements can usually be forecast allowing operational planning activities to predict and build the gains into the medium- and long-term forecasts.

For example, if the output of a machine is to be improved by 6% over three months, by monitoring the progress towards the goal, planners can begin to work with the forecasted output rates when putting schedules together.

Sequence improvements; improvements in one activity have a spin-off effect on another part of the organisation. By working together, separate activities can combine the results of their efforts and maximise collaborative improvements.

Control and monitoring of performance; monitoring the performance of the activities can provide valuable information on the effect of the changes. The higher the detail, the more beneficial the information becomes.

Such data can be used to anticipate when targets and milestone will be reached, which is useful for financial control and planning.

Often the improvements require a level of expenditure to make them happen – new equipment, training, or development costs, for example.

By monitoring the performance, it is possible to anticipate when the required finances might be available to fund a particular project or improvement activity.

Cascaded targets and tasks that everyone understands.

Management should realise when the head announces to the organisation "FurnFast will diversify into complementary markets and products, which should account for over 10% of the new sales revenue", few individuals understand the full impact of what was said. Fewer individuals realise **they** are going to make these planned changes.

By cascading the objective through the various levels of the organisation, at each level, it can be translated into words individuals understand. Then it can be converted into targets and tasks for everyone to complete.

This process makes everyone feel like they are an essential part of one big team working on one big project.

One Vision–One Plan–One Big Team; by measuring the progress of the big project (the objective), the performance of individuals is also being monitored.

The monitoring can provide a significant boost to individual morale by being part of something important; it creates a sense of belonging.

Defined structure and responsibilities; as we've already touched upon briefly, this methodology forces organisations to re-assess the organisational structure and, in some cases, to redefine the duties of individuals. It provides an opportunity to look at the organisation with a fresh pair of eyes and to determine who does what.

I've got dozens of stories to tell about individuals working in organisations, who don't have a proper job and often don't fit into the structure; they still get paid though.

Measuring success; we've already established that monitoring is essential to the success of this methodology; if we report a target has been reached, we can celebrate the achievement. Every time!

Define the baseline

At the outset, management must define the baseline or the current level of performance.

The baseline is the starting point for all future performance trends. Figure Three shows a typical performance trend graph. The trend starts at the baseline, i.e. as the change gets underway.

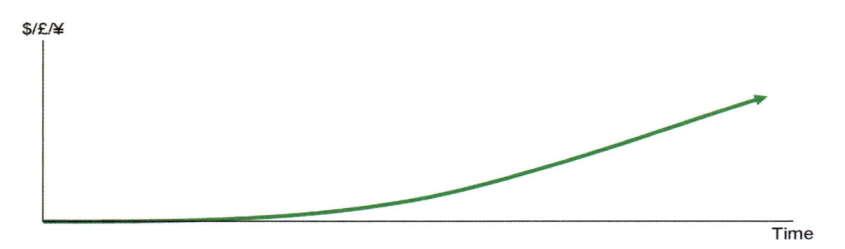

Figure Three: Performance trend

The organisation should measure progress relative to the baseline position. The baseline might be the current sales revenue, for example, or the number of customers, or some other indicator of current performance.

Monitor and report progress on completion of each task, in relation to the baseline and, most importantly, keep the project under control and moving forward.

Throughout any change activity, maintaining operational control is essential; such control relies on constant feedback on progress. An organisation is like a supertanker; it moves forward with great force and takes a massive amount of effort to stop it or to make it change direction. By taking measurements at infrequent or long intervals, the organisation has less time to react to poor performance or undesirable trends. Regular and frequent information is required so adjustments can be made to the direction of the organisation.

I worked with a company which measured and reported sales every month, and they thought it was adequate, I also worked with an organisation which measured and reported sales daily, and they felt it was not enough.

Take measurements that allow sufficient understanding and control of the activity. In our fictitious organisation, which I'll introduce soon, only the head and the directors can determine what needs to be measured to maintain control.

I recently worked with a global organisation which was eager to increase the number of its non-UK customers. The top management assumed the number of customers, whether domestic or global, was a measure of success; to them, more overseas customers equalled more income and profit. However, soon, they began to realise that global customers didn't spend as much as domestic customers and cost more to service. The global growth was adversely affecting profitability and the support to domestic customers.

It is vital to measure and report what is critical to the success of the organisation. In this example, there was a strong correlation between the higher number of global customers, the forecasted increase in income (which never arrived), and a resulting reduction in profit. Clearly, there was a lack of understanding of the organisation and its customers.

Is this book for you?

Naturally, this book is suitable for anyone involved in the development, definition and delivery of strategy, especially those people who are also charged with effecting change.

Typically, you have a *RESPONSIBILITY*.

Executive	*Director*	*Charge-hand*	*Chief*
Founder	*Leader*	*Organiser*	*Partner*
Owner	*Principal*	*Dean*	*Boss*
CEO	*Captain*	*Controller*	*President*
Manager	*Supervisor*	*MD*	*Consultant*

For the whole or part of an *ORGANISATION*.

Bus	*Circle*	*Association*	*Foundation*
Firm	*Faculty*	*Garage*	*Concern*
Store	*Party*	*Vessel*	*Business*
Band	*Co-operative*	*Institution*	*Corporation*
Section	*Office*	*Society*	*Train*
Ship	*Plant*	*Company*	*Hotel*
Practice	*Granary*	*Outfit*	*Shop*
Government	*Alliance*	*Department*	*Club*
Church	*Camp*	*Partnership*	*Union*

This book is aimed at anyone who has the *RESPONSIBILITY* for the whole or part of any *ORGANISATION*.

"Good past performance is not a guarantee of good future performance."

This book is especially useful to people who are responsible for planning and managing change through projects, improvements, initiatives, plans, and so on.

Throughout the book, I refer to terms that are mainly suited to manufacturing – the book is based on the issues facing FurnFast, our fictitious manufacturing company. However, the content and processes described within are equally applicable to any organisation. So, when I mention customers, for example, I could be talking about members or pupils, and so on. Equally, widgets could be ebooks or insurance policies or anything.

Photograph Three: This book is aimed at YOU

Review:
What did we learn in the Introduction?

- Organisations need solid foundations on which to build; workers provide those foundations.

- Plans are developed and effectively communicated from the top, but the actions start at the bottom (the foundation) and build upwards.

- When the head of an organisation announces changes are going be made, most of the organisation don't understand what it means to them, their job, their role, and their earnings.

- Often when the head of an organisation makes an announcement about changes, the employees hear nothing but rumours.

- Measure and report what is critical to the success of the organisation.

- Report the progress on completion of every task; regular information is required so minor adjustments can be made to the plan.

- The advantage of this approach is the effective management of change.

In Section 1, we learn how we can prepare for change.

Section One

Setting the scene: All Change!

Definitions: *All - completely*
Change - to make different

Change

Today, more than ever, organisations are operating in an environment which is ever-changing. The changes, mostly driven by external factors, require those organisations, and all the individuals within them, to accept the need to change.

Whether we like it, or not, change is inevitable.

Unfortunately, change often brings a sense of insecurity, perception of risk, and mistrust of those imposing the changes.

Changing something usually means the outcome is unwelcome and risky, even though it may promise, and lead to, improvement. Individuals can often react with resentment and resistance if changes are forced upon them; it's a natural response to the unknown.

However, we live on a tiny planet in the throes of a communication revolution; where markets are global. Consumers can buy anything from anywhere in the world via the internet.

Organisations are no longer competing with companies in the same town; the *new* competitors, who are promising bigger, better, cheaper, and faster, products and services, are spread throughout the world.

For organisations to survive the future, they must seek and welcome change. Those changes must be planned from the top and executed from the bottom.

Market position

Some organisations believe they can maintain their market position by making small evolutionary changes to their operation; they think steady growth year-on-year should be enough.

Their Business Plan shows a modest 2-3% increase in turnover for the next 12 months – *more of the same*.

The reality is this; it's tough competing in a global market, and it's going to get much tougher.

As organisations begin to realise that significant change is required to allow them to compete in a worldwide market, they're developing their Business Plans accordingly.

Unfortunately, some organisations are not even achieving modest targets (a 2-3% increase in turnover). Their Business Plan is just not robust enough to beat the competition. Evolutionary growth cannot compete against strong competitors with revolutionary intentions.

Historically, many organisations have been content with modest growth year after year. To survive, organisations need to aim much higher, to be ambitious, and to succeed.

Consider what your competitors could be planning; how will they continue to grow?

Will your competitors be looking for:

- new and emerging markets,
- new products and services,
- increasing their market share or
- taking customers from your organisation?

Organisations can no longer afford to think about evolution – they must think of revolution.

Avoid over-reacting

Reacting to every market trend is like a young fox trying to catch a chicken. The fox chases one chicken for a few seconds and realises it's not making progress; it turns and chases another for a few more seconds, but soon recognises it's too slow. Again, the fox turns and puts even more effort into catching yet another chicken, but to no avail.

A lot of effort for no gain.

Stop!

Evaluate the competitors, assess the market conditions, and embrace the new technology. Consider how the organisation might change, how it could compete in a tougher market, and then determine the new objective for the future.

PESTLE is a useful management tool to assess current conditions.

POLITICAL

ECONOMICAL

SOCIAL

TECHNOLOGICAL

LEGAL

ENVIRONMENTAL

The PESTLE evaluation is a valuable exercise and very effective use of management resource. Carefully consider, step-by-step, what the organisation needs to change in order to grow.

The purpose of the PESTLE exercise is to establish the basis for the strategy and the business plan; it also ensures everyone understands their role in making the changes to achieve the strategy. More on PESTLE later.

Look at the bigger picture, research the technological trends, determine where the market is going, assess what the competitors are doing, forecast what customers might be asking for in future, consider the organisation's strengths and weaknesses, and decide what needs to change:

- Where is the organisation now?
- Where does the organisation need to be?
- What needs to change?
- How will the change be made?

Planning overview

Planning is a critical part of the successful management of change. In the initial stage of the planning process, organisations determine where they are now, and where they want to be.

Planning sounds simple, but it requires some intelligent and focussed thought if the plan is to be meaningful. Planning is about mapping the journey; it's similar to a route plan which ensures you get to your destination. When the plan is complete, it needs to be checked to make sure it's SMART.

After the plan is approved, it's time to start the transition and to implement the required changes. As the plan is executed, the progress must be monitored and reported on a regular formal basis at first. As the project becomes embedded in the day-to-day activities, the reporting aspect will become part of what individuals do.

If the organisation doesn't make sufficient progress according to the plan, or it decides it wants to do something else, alter the plan, it's flexible; it's just a plan. Above all else, make sure the plan shows the links between each task.

Changing a task will often have a significant effect on another task or even on the entire project. Ensure that everyone is updated on any changes to the plan.

More on planning in Section Two.

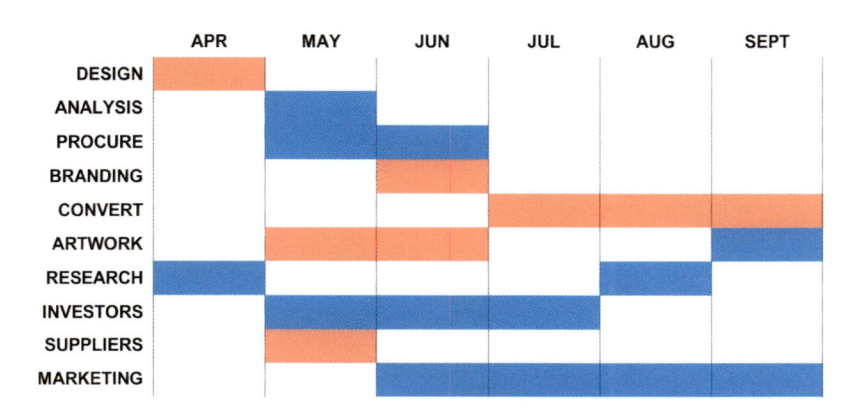

Figure Four: Example of a Project Plan

How organisations grow

Organisations tend to grow in phases. Much has been written about the various stages of development, and what organisations should expect at each. Organisations differ and, while there are similarities in behaviour patterns between growing organisations, management determines what happens during each phase of the growth.

Imagine a young growing organisation, still full of the excitement of the launch, flourishing on the prospect of growth. The team is small, unstructured, and very hard working. The workers are keen to develop the processes to match the ever-changing circumstances. Their objective is the establishment of the business. Communication is easy amongst the few employees; their job roles are flexible, and there is a great team spirit.

As the organisation grows, and the workforce expands, verbal communication across the entire company is no longer possible, other methods of communication are adopted. Some individuals begin to feel neglected – why do they no longer have day to day contact with the boss? Individuals are still keen, but turnover per person is steadily falling. The primary focus is the growth of the organisation.

The organisation continues to flourish and begins to achieve some success. The workforce further expands, but turnover per person falls further. There are many reasons for this; individuals are not as committed as when the company first started, individuals are no longer motivated to get the organisation established, and there is no longer a clear focus.

Morale starts to fall; some individuals resign and leave, but are quickly replaced by employees who weren't around in the early days.

Everyone, except the customer, has become absorbed in their role and is not looking at the bigger picture.

Customers are the first to notice diminishing levels of service quality. Unfortunately, they can no longer talk directly to the people who started the organisation; to the same people who fostered the working relationship with the customers. Little by little, the customers drift away.

The organisation has options:
1) It can continue as before and hope performance improves,
2) It can put measures in place to address some of the issues, or
3) It can take a fresh look at what it's doing, where it's going, and where it wants to be. Then plan to make the necessary changes.

Option one is too risky, and it only serves to delay the failure of the organisation.

If the company chooses option two, continues to grow and begins to address some of the issues, it will find it will become less flexible when it finally realises it needs to change. Not only that, the managers will no longer be innovators; they will lose their keen edge due to the day-to-day humdrum of tackling problems.

Option three is the most difficult, but not the most painful in the longer term. It requires effort, and it needs drive, determination, and a clear focus. If planned and implemented successfully, option three will secure the future of the organisation.

Let's go back and revisit our scenario:

Imagine a growing organisation, full of the excitement of being a market leader, flourishing on its growth.

The team is keen, structured, and very hard working.

The workers continue to improve the processes to match the ever-changing circumstances. Their objective is the growth and success of the organisation.

Communication is easy amongst the many activities, job roles are flexible, and there is a great team spirit across the growing number of employees.

Measures of success

How do you gauge the success of your organisation?

The profit?

The level of sales?

The percentage of market share?

The number of outlets?

The number of customers?

The number of employees?

The measure of the success of any organisation must be a significant component of its objective. The objective is the essential element of the Business Plan. For example, if sales revenue is the measure of success, the aim must be to increase sales revenue.

The Business Plan must consider the significant elements that affect the objective.

In our example, the goal is: "FurnFast will diversify into complementary markets and products, which should account for over 10% of the new sales revenue". However, if the costs rise in order to diversify, the organisation is not going to make any profit.

So, the Business Plan must include tasks to increase sales, maintain profits, lower costs, raise productivity, reduce waste, and launch new products, etc.

It is imperative that organisations develop a process which ensures any undesirable results or trends in the achievement of the objective, are immediately escalated to the management for action.

There is no point in working hard to achieve something which is having a detrimental effect on the organisation.

Being realistic

Any changes made in any area of an organisation will affect activities in other areas of the organisation, and maybe activities outside the organisation too. Changes to processes or products in one department can cause problems in other departments, and possibly more serious issues within the product or service pipeline.

All the planned changes must be researched, discussed, and agreed, before implementation.

The process of cascading the objectives and tasks throughout the organisation must take consideration of the likely (and sometimes unlikely) effects of the changes.

Don't try to make plans for the next ten years. A five-year strategy is a dream, a three-year plan is a vision, a one-year plan is an intention, but a one-month project is a reality – it's a *to-do* list, and it's immediate.

It's a good idea to have the longer-term (five-year or three-year) vision but concentrate on the one-year plan and especially on what needs to be done next month and next week.

The costs of failure

"The organisation just wasn't ready for such a major change."

is just like saying,

"Management wasn't able to understand and communicate the changes."

An organisation is a group of individuals with a common objective. If the objective is *common,* then all individuals should understand what the aim is, they can then show commitment, and appreciate how they can contribute to achieving the goal.

Figure Five: Plans and activities

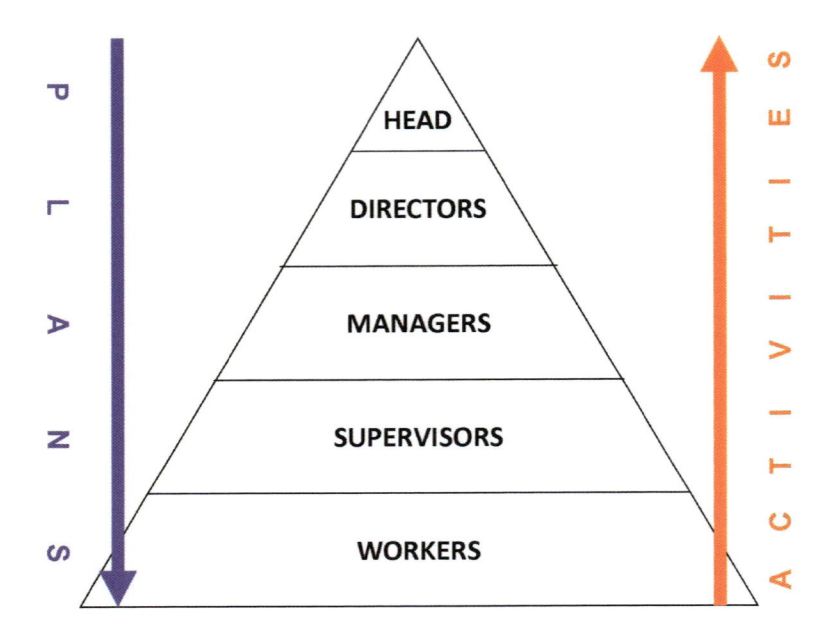

PLANS ← → ACTIVITIES

- HEAD
- DIRECTORS
- MANAGERS
- SUPERVISORS
- WORKERS

Unfortunately, change initiatives fail regularly. There are many reasons for this, and most relate to failings or misunderstandings at the management level. Many managers don't realise it's the workers who make the changes, not the management.

So, to manage any change, management must tell each person what the organisation is going to do and get them to work towards achieving the shared objective. Often organisations issue glib statements about a new initiative and just expect everyone to get involved, it's never so easy.

Start with a clear vision of where the organisation needs to be; more on this later.

Effective management

In many ways, I'm unforgiving when it comes to the subject of management ability. Anyone working in a managerial position should have a range of management skills, including:

- Finance,
- Planning,
- Communication,
- Leadership,
- Problem-solving,
- Reporting,
- Decision making,
- People,
- Negotiation,
- IT
- Leadership.

Plus, a manager should be able to organise and run productive meetings, manage time, deliver briefings, and control projects.

Before organisations begin to consider any changes, or start to think about planning for the changes, they need to get the management team on the same page, thinking about the organisation, understanding the organisation, and sufficiently motivated to make the changes; often retraining is required.

The primary *management tools* are useful, but in my experience, they are frequently misused because the user has not been adequately trained on the correct use of a particular tool.

Be aware of the manager who attempts to use the same management tool in every circumstance.

This list is not exhaustive, but highlights some of the tools which may be useful in the management of change:

- **Statistical Process Control**   Controlling processes

- **Pareto Analysis**   Problem-analysis

- **Failure Mode & Effect Analysis**   Risk reduction

- **Cause and Effect Analysis**   Problem solving

- **Process Mapping**   Improvement

I'm not going to get into the details of how to use each tool, although I do need to stress these tools can be dangerous if misused, so only allow competent individuals to use them.

When a roadside mechanic arrives to fix a car, he doesn't begin by emptying the entire contents of his toolbox onto the road and attempt to use each tool to fix the problem. He selects the tool he needs and uses it skillfully to do the job. It's the same with the management tools; the user should identify the correct tool and use it efficiently.

The Management of Change is the subject of many books, most explain what should be done, but they seldom describe how it should be done. The *how* is important.

So that's possibly part of the problem. Organisations often want to be told what to do; for them, it's the easy option. However, consider the old proverb about teaching a man to fish. It's more worthwhile to show someone than to do it for them.

There are no formulas, templates or secrets for managing change. Each market is unique, each organisation is unique, and each employee is unique. Therefore, when the head of the organisation, in conjunction with the directors, decides to make the organisation successful, they must develop and communicate a revolutionary Business Plan that will change the way everyone in the organisation works.

The management of change begins with an objective. Unfortunately, the objective is often decided before managers get involved.

In other words, the changes have been agreed at the highest level, and so now they just need to be implemented.

I've seen a lot of evidence of this; where the decisions have been made without any consultation with the people who do the work on a day-to-day basis.

This is like building pyramids from the top. The directors can't do the tasks; they MUST rely on the workers. The directors can't build the organisation from the top.

By imposing the changes and timescales upon the organisation, the project is wholly misunderstood; as a result, there is:

- No obvious reason to make the changes
- No motivation to make the changes
- No leadership to lead the changes
- No communication about the changes
- No perceived benefit of the changes, and
- **No chance of the objective being achieved.**

In this type of scenario - one that is common - the organisation just scored an own goal. Management is frustrated, the workforce is confused, and the customers are concerned.

Bad Move!

Before getting started

Have you ever wondered what heads of other organisations want from their workers?

- Do they know?

- Can they define it?

- Have they defined it?

- Have they explained it to everyone?

How can the head of an organisation expect the workers to do the right thing if the workers have not been advised or trained?

Simply, the head of an organisation must tell the workers what to do by using the structure of the organisation to deliver the message.

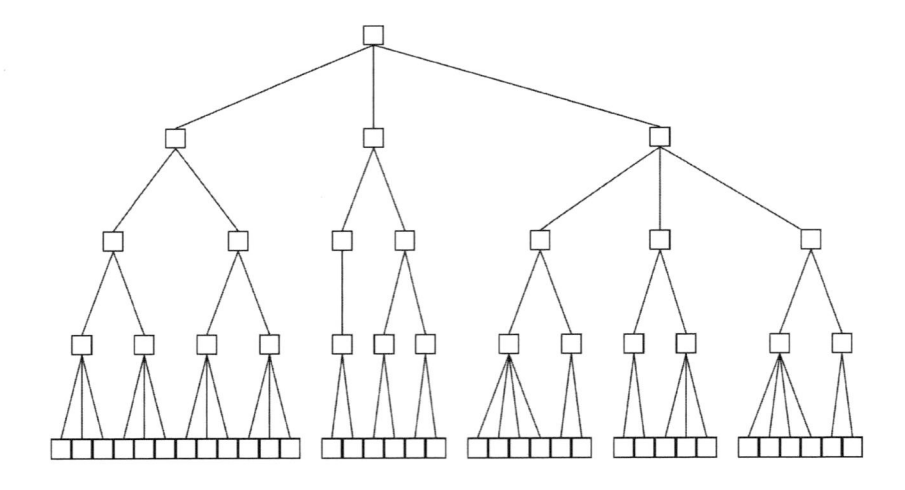

Figure Six: Communication structure

In Figure Six, we see the organisational structure we saw in the Introduction. Using the same arrangement, the head of the organisation can consistently communicate with the entire workforce. The head of the organisation can make an announcement which will be heard by all.

However, it's not quite so easy, as we shall soon see.

I often describe the similarities between a Business Plan and a route plan. Without a plan, the individuals must follow the head of the organisation; they only need to do what they're told to do. The leader must be available 24/7 to tell the workers what to do. Without the head, the workers would be lost. In this scenario, no-one except the head needs to think; therefore, this approach is never going to work.

Steve Jobs, the former Apple CEO, once said,

"It doesn't make sense to hire smart people and tell them what to do; we hire smart people so they can tell us what to do."

Without a plan, the workers will find they begin to work against each other instead of with each other; there will be conflict.

Any planned objective or task must be shared with everyone (it's not as easy as it sounds), then all individuals will know precisely where the organisation is heading and will join the head of the organisation on the *journey*.

To involve the workers, management needs to outline the benefits of the changes and what it means to the organisation and the individuals.

The head needs to gain support at the highest level and cascade the objective to the next level down; the cascade process is where detail is added to the plan. The plan brings management together and gets them thinking about the organisation as a whole.

Section two of this book covers planning in more detail.

Review:
What did we learn in Section 1?

- Change is inevitable. Unfortunately, it often brings a sense of insecurity, perception of risk, and mistrust of those imposing the changes.

- Organisations can no longer afford to think evolution – they must think of revolution.

- Research the technological trends, determine where the market is going, assess what the competitors are doing, consider the organisation's strengths and weaknesses, then decide what needs to change.

- It's vital to get the management team thinking about the organisation, understanding the organisation, and motivated to make the changes – often retraining is required.

- The head of an organisation must communicate by using the structure of the organisation to deliver the message.

- Organisations must develop a process which ensures any undesirable results are immediately escalated to the Management for action. There is no point in working hard to achieve something which is having a detrimental effect on the organisation.

In Section 2, we introduce the cascading process to demonstrate how the head of the organisation ensures the message is understood by everyone.

Section Two

Planning the Changes!

Definitions: *Planning - preparing a scheme*
Change - to make something different

Organisations need a plan

Organisations need an objective, a vision, an intention, an aim, a target, a goal, or a purpose.

The title of the plan is not important; organisations can call it whatever they want, the key is that it should provide focus, show what the objective is, and describe how it will be met.

Without a plan, there's no direction; organisations, and the individuals within them, simply don't know where they're heading. Of course, it's essential for an organisation to have a Business Plan, but the plan must be communicated, understood, and implemented.

Many organisations really struggle with the implementation phase, which causes many initiatives to fail. The problem lies not with the implementation; the problem is the plan itself.

Suitably detailed Business Plans are much easier to implement, especially if the methodology described in this book is adopted.

Implementation of a Business Plan is not a separate process; it's part of the overall organisational activity.

A good Business Plan will detail the tasks which have to be completed to achieve the objective. It's the level of detail that allows the plan to be implemented.

Through a fictitious organisation – FurnFast – and various scenarios, this book will demonstrate how to develop and implement a Business Plan that will achieve the objective.

The pitfalls of Business Plans

Before we get too far into the detail of what a Business Plan should contain, and how we might begin developing a great plan, I want to highlight and explain some of the pitfalls of Business Plans.

When developing a Business Plan, it is necessary to decide what the plan will contain.

We must start by considering who might use the plan:

Management?
    Customers?
        Workers?
            Investors?
                Suppliers?

Realistically, each of these groups could use the Business Plan; the plan needs to be structured and phrased so that every individual understands it.

Some common pitfalls of Business Plans are:

- **The Business Plan could be poorly written, lacking detail and ill-conceived** showing that management isn't serious about the future of the organisation. A Business Plan requires time and effort for it to be correctly composed.

- **The Business Plan could be too general** to suit any activity or individual. A quick internet search reveals thousands of off-the-shelf plans and templates – avoid these. A Business Plan must be specific to the organisation.

- **The Business Plan could be too ambiguous and open to interpretation.** There must be no room for misinterpretation of the plan – spell it out clearly.

    The changes, when implemented, will not be useful if the Business Plan doesn't detail the tasks to be completed.

- **The Business Plan could have no defined targets**, so the workers don't know what they're aiming for and, more importantly, they won't realise they've hit (or missed) the target.

    Where possible, use performance measures, such as Key Performance Indicators (KPIs) to define critical milestones.

- **The Business Plan could have no timescales**, so the workers don't know how long they've got to make the changes.

    The lack of deadlines can create a much more significant problem of scheduling of tasks. It's pointless scheduling a significant product launch months before the new product is available.

    Timescales allow for the structuring of the plan to deliver the outcomes in the right order.

- **The Business Plan could be unambitious – not challenging.**

    The problem with a Business Plan that doesn't create sufficient change is people get bored, the organisation loses market position, and then sales start to fall.

    Aim for something which will, at least, get the organisation thinking and talking about change.

    What is worse? Aiming high and falling short of the target or aiming low and hitting the target?

- **The Business Plan could be incomprehensible.** If individuals are not able to understand the plan, they're not going to get eagerly involved and make the changes. I've seen Business Plans which didn't make sense; they were just too confusing.

The Business Plan could be confidential. I've seen this too often; where the Business Plan is for management only. If the management wants to implement changes and expect the organisation to do something, why not tell everyone?

Management should make the plan available for everyone to see. If it's not practical or possible, then ensure everyone has access to the elements of the plan that affect them.

Business planning

> **Furnfast Business Plan**
>
> **CONFIDENTIAL**

Beware of any Business Plan marked CONFIDENTIAL; consider the purpose of such a document.

Who is it for?

More importantly, who is it being hidden from?

Business planning is the most essential activity any organisation undertakes. It is imperative that a Business Plan is developed and fully implemented. Without a good plan, the organisation and the individuals within it will carry on doing what they've always done.

An imperfect plan could lead to failure, especially if lots of effort and resource are used in its implementation.

A good Business Plan is easier to implement than a bad one because the plan includes checks which monitor the completion of the tasks and the achievement of the objective.

However, it's not enough to just develop a first-rate Business Plan. The plan must then be communicated to everyone using a language they understand.

Every individual in the organisation has a vital part to play in making the changes happen. Management is asking everyone to do something different, so each person must understand what it is they need to do.

By cascading the objective into the organisation and translating it into tasks, it is possible to visualise the achievement of the objective. At the task level, it is also possible to identify the individuals who will be responsible for undertaking the tasks, how much it might cost, and how long it will take. Therefore, we can prepare a detailed project plan.

The time taken to develop a sound Business Plan which details the full cascade from the objective to the tasks, and gets agreement at every level in the cascade, is around 6-18 weeks depending on the size and complexity of the organisation.

EXERCISE

If you have a Business Plan, find it, and read it thoroughly. Does it contain any of the pitfalls listed here?

- Is the Business Plan, or an extract from it, available to all employees? YES/NO
- Is the Business Plan written in a language all employees can understand? YES/NO
- Does the Business Plan contain more than one page of financial information? YES/NO
    - If so, is the information able to be understood by all employees? YES/NO
- Are all the targets clearly defined? YES/NO
- Has the overall timeframe for the delivery of the Business Plan been defined? YES/NO
    - If so, is everyone aware of it? YES/NO

The purpose of this exercise is to highlight the common and basic mistakes I find with Business Plans. I often wonder if Business Plans are simply written for the sake of creating something which attempts to look impressive.

It seems that, in some cases, there is no connection between the plan and the activities, and, in such circumstances, the plan is never going to be implemented – it's just a paper exercise.

In reality, the Business Plan is the only opportunity an organisation gets to review what it's doing, where it's going, and what it might consider doing instead.

The Cascading Structure

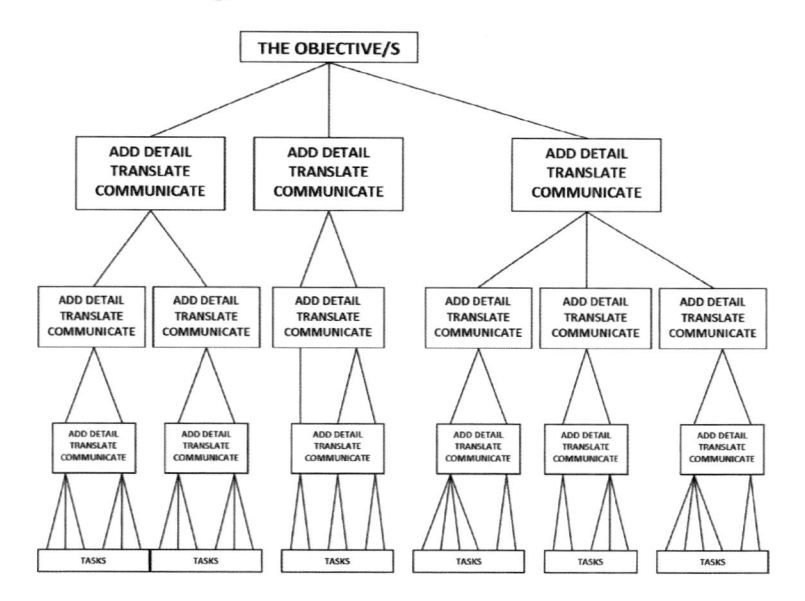

Figure Seven: Cascading structure

The cascading structure shown here looks remarkably like the organisational structure and the communication structure we've already seen.

Of course, it's the same structure!

At each level in the structure, from top to bottom, the message acquires detail, is translated into something understandable, and communicated – we'll look at the Cascading Process later.

The Plan

Managers generally consider themselves to be good at planning, though many might admit they're not good at implementing those plans.

Poor implementation is deemed to be the cause of more failures than a worthless Business Plan.

Poor implementation is a direct result of poor planning.

Here's a simple example; suppose we're in Central Park Zoo, NY, and we want to go to Madison Square Garden, NY, which of these would be most useful: 1 or 2?

1.
Present Location: Central Park Zoo

Destination: Madison Square Garden

Head South via 5th Ave for 1.3 miles
Turn R onto W 39th for 0.4 miles
Turn L onto 7th Ave for 0.3 miles

2.

Destination: Madison Square Garden

There is a lot of difference between the two sets of information in this example.

The first set is undoubtedly the most useful since it provides turn-by-turn instructions and distances.

The second set gives us the destination only.

This example might seem to be meaningless but, in reality, millions of organisations have Business Plans which state the objective only. Having a destination (or goal) is useful, but how is the organisation going to get there?

A Business Plan is like a route plan; it allows the organisation to get from where it is now (the baseline) to where it wants it to be (the objective).

The plan must contain sufficient detail, similar to a Route Plan, showing every turn, direction, and distance, to the next waypoint. We can then use the Business Plan to measure the progress towards the objective.

By monitoring progress, it is possible to answer fundamental questions:

- How close are we to the objective?
- How are we going to get there?
- When are we going to get there?
- Are we working together?
- Are we going to lose someone along the way?
- How much is it costing?

The planning process begins with a statement of the objective and ends with the achievement of the objective.

The implementation phase is an essential part of the overall business planning process. Additionally, the detail in the Business Plan drives the implementation phase. In other words, the Business Plan must have sufficient detail to allow the implementation; the details come from the cascade.

Plans can change

Gone are the days of keeping a detailed Business Plan in the bottom drawer of a desk or securely filed away in a cupboard. The plan should be a living entity which details everything organisations (and individuals) will do.

In one company I worked with, at the end of the business planning process (lasting about three months), the managing director thanked everyone who was involved in the process. Just as he was ending his impromptu speech, he paused and looked around at the print-out of the new Business Plan adorning the four walls of the meeting room.

Then came the warning, "We've planned what we're going to do to ensure our success, it's here on this chart; don't do **anything** unless it's on the plan. Thank you."

A brave move, in my estimation. I met with the managing director later in the day and asked him about his parting shot.

"It's a plan", he explained, "and plans can be changed. If someone can justify changing it, I welcome their input and it will be considered. But I don't want anyone doing their own thing and not following the plan."

It's true; it's a plan, and it can be amended. However, those amendments need to follow a process to determine how they might affect the entire organisation.

It's OK to modify the plan as long as the consequences are known; it's a changing world, plans must be flexible.

Business Plan or Route Plan

As I stated, in many ways, it is useful to draw comparisons between a Business Plan and a Route Plan.

We've ascertained that a Business Plan takes account of where the organisation is now (let's call it Point A) and where it wants to be (let's call it Point B).

The plan must also detail the actions required to get the organisation from A to B.

A route plan does precisely that; it shows people how to get from where they are now (Central Park Zoo, New York) to where they want to be (Madison Square Garden, New York).

As the detail of the route plan increases, the higher is the likelihood of reaching the destination (or the goal). Likewise, if the detail of the Business Plan increases, the higher the prospect of the organisation achieving the objective.

There is a spin-off advantage of adding detail to a Business Plan; the details come from the discussions with the people who have the responsibility for delivering the plan, such as managers, supervisors and workers.

By getting them involved in the process of adding detail, it confirms that they understand the objectives, and it shows a commitment to their achievement.

Not only that, the managers, supervisors and workers know a lot more about their job than you do; so use that expertise to identify where improvements can be made, for example.

Above all, don't try to impose changes without having discussions, or without a full understanding and commitment of everyone involved.

Attempting to change a process is impossible without the buy-in from the people who use the process every day. It's important to get them on your side.

And it's not too difficult. Explain that the organisation is going to change, make sure they understand how it might affect them, gain their trust, get their commitment, and use their experience to define and make the changes.

Heads of organisations must ensure the Business Plan doesn't hold them back, and that it continues to support the achievement of the objective.

Let's go back to our example; we were in Central Park Zoo, and we wanted to go to Madison Square Garden. With the detailed route plan, it was relatively easy to get from A to B without too much fuss.

However, supposing we were in the Central Park Zoo, New York, and we wanted to go to Golden Gate Park, San Francisco; can you imagine the size and detail of the route plan.

Well, here it is:

Present Location: Central Park Zoo, NY

Destination: Golden Gate Park, SF

Head SW on 5th Ave toward E 64th St for 56 ft

Turn L onto E 64th St for 0.1 miles

Turn L onto Madison Ave for 0.1 miles

Turn L onto E 66th St for 0.1 miles

Continue onto 65th St Transverse for 0.6 miles

Continue onto W 66th St for 0.6 miles

Turn R onto Riverside Blvd for 0.3 miles

Turn L onto the NY 9A/Henry Hudson Pkwy for 4.7 miles

Take exit 14 for I-95 at W 178 St for 0.4 miles

Keep right at the fork onto I-95 Lower Level S for 2.1 miles

Continue onto I-95 for 0.2 miles

Keep R to continue on I-95 S for 2.5 miles

Keep R to continue on I-80 W for 2901.7 miles

Take exit 1B to merge onto US-101 N for 1.1 miles

Continue onto Octavia Blvd for 0.3 miles

Turn L onto Fell St for 1.3 miles

That's a lot of detail, but it's not the full picture.

Imagine what sort of plan would be required if each person needed a unique route plan because they're not all coming from the same starting point.

For people in an organisation, where every individual has a unique role, each person needs a unique set of instructions.

That gives us some indication of the size of the plan; we're not looking at One-Business-Plan-Fits-All.

Instead, we're looking at one strategy which will be tailored to each person in the organisation.

For example, let us go back to the guy operating the machine and our example objective; "*FurnFast will diversify into complementary markets and products, which should account for over 10% of the new sales revenue*" probably means he will have little involvement in making any changes initially.

However, in the technical department, the designers might have to design new products. Similarly, in the marketing department, the salespeople will have to sell the new products. So, it's the same objective for everyone, but each has a unique set of tasks to achieve the target.

Likewise, as we just mentioned, the objective is to get to Golden Gate Park in San Francisco, but each person has a different starting point, which gives us some indication of the size and detail of a realistic plan. Everyone needs a unique plan; otherwise, each might end up in a different place.

The Business Plan is the organisation's guide; the organisation is about to go to an unfamiliar place, so develop a detailed plan.

The best plans have the right level of detail and prove to be most effective. An effective Business Plan must include everyone and everything that impacts on the organisation.

We have determined that a good Business Plan needs to illustrate:

- where the organisation is now (the baseline),
- where it wants to be (the objective) and
- a route plan of how it's going to get there (the tasks).

We haven't yet considered when it will get there (time).

Timing is crucial, especially where tasks have to be completed in sequence.

Simply, a timescale must be set, which allows everyone to reach the objective at the same time. Time also introduces a sense of urgency and priority in getting the tasks completed.

Missions and Visions

I'm not going to get bogged down with semantics about Mission Statements, Vision Statements, Value Statements, and so on; it's not important what the *statement* is called, but there needs to be a form of words which tells EVERYONE where the organisation wants to be in relation to where it is now.

For example, we could say:

"To be Europe's leading provider of widgets."

This *statement* should also include some key factors which add sufficient detail to the overall statement to make it SMART. Invariably, the key objective is to maintain or grow the organisation, which often requires income. Therefore, the "statement" should include financial measures:

"To be Europe's leading provider of widgets with profitable annual income in excess of £120 million in 2025."

For the sake of putting a title to this *statement*, we shall call it our Prime Objective – it forms the basis of the strategy.

Introducing the Prime Objective

The Prime Objective is the single most important statement; it captures the strategic goals and targets and summarises them in one proclamation.

It is often a personal message from the most senior person for the benefit of individuals, suppliers, shareholders, and customers alike.

The agreed Prime Objective needs to be broken down into groups of tasks, which will form the core of the Business Plan.

The process of developing the plan would typically take several weeks, or months, depending on the size of the organisation and the type of activity it's involved in.

The directors determine how the Prime Objective will be achieved; the output from that process forms the strategy.

Each director then defines how the strategy will be achieved. The output from the process is a set of goals. Those goals are explained to the managers, and an agreement is established on how the goals will be met.

Each manager then goes to the supervisors and explains how each goal will be realised.

Each supervisor then goes to the workers and discusses the goals, seeking valuable input from the worker and gaining a commitment to the *objective*.

More detail is added at each stage; a crucial part of the communication is determining how the targets (strategy, goals, tasks will be achieved).

We'll see the cascade in action in Section 4.

Rules for Business Plans

Business Plans are usually written to cover a period of three to five years; a good plan is for life and should continue to evolve as the organisation grows.

Depending on the nature of its activities and the environment in which the organisation operates, it's hard to plan three years into the future with any degree of certainty. The plan must be fluid; it should be amended to suit market forces, new technologies, customer trends, etc.

If the Business Plan isn't changed, the organisation will eventually suffer. A three-year or five-year strategy should be reviewed and converted into a one-year plan annually. Where possible, concentrate on the short-term plans; turn them into *To-Do lists*.

At all costs, avoid making bland statements in Business Plans:

> *"Enhance revenues through the development of activities in the Business Lines."*

I've actually seen this in a Business Plan. It's not a plan – it's waffle. What activities? Enhance by how much? By what date? Who's responsible? At what cost?

Be more precise. Such weak statements are like declaring:

> *"We will make more money by doing things differently."*

Some organisations put a lot of effort into their Business Plan to make it look slick and professional when presented to the directors, the management team, or other stakeholders.

The Business Plan is for the organisation to get them from Point A to Point B. If the plan is going to be presented to the owners or other stakeholders, then that's a separate exercise. Get the content right before it's made to look attractive.

Consider the outside factors which might influence the organisation in the coming months and years, make assumptions and append them to the plan.

Take account of market forecasts, consider raw material prices, and assess the emerging technology; how will they directly/indirectly affect the organisation?

As we stated earlier, a Business Plan, written and approved at *director level* would be meaningless when passed to the *worker level*. I've seen this many, many times.

Why publish a plan to individuals in an organisation if, to them, the content is incomprehensible?

That is the key to a good Business Plan; it must be understood at every level of the organisation, so every element of the plan can cascade down through the organisation. The cascading process adds the required detail relating to each department, operation and individual.

The crux of this technique is that everyone is expected to understand the plan. Likewise, the plan should provide the detail required to deliver the strategy.

The top level of the Business Plan will have around a dozen strategic targets the directors have agreed. By cascading the objectives into the organisation, the plan is translated into hundreds of tasks everyone can understand and undertake.

How many organisations can honestly say they don't need to change?

So why aren't they changing?

PESTLE

We briefly mentioned PESTLE in Section 1, introducing it as a useful management tool to assess the current external conditions.

PESTLE is an acronym: Political, Economic, Social, Technological, Legal and Environmental.

There is no right or wrong way of completing a PESTLE analysis of an organisation and the arena in which it operates.

It often involves a deep understanding of the political, economic, social, technological, legal and environmental framework which has, or may have, an impact on the organisation – directly or indirectly.

If the required knowledge is not available from within the organisation, outside support should be sought to find answers to critical questions.

Use PESTLE as a framework for the study, considering and researching the factors for each element in turn.

Look for current conditions and potential factors in the future. Be aware of new environmental legislation, for example. Below is a set of example factors for each PESTLE condition. Consider the positives and negatives of each element. What could help and what could hinder the organisation?

Political: Tax, Trade, Government, Tariffs, Education, Immigration

Economical: Inflation, Interest, Growth, Exchange, Price, Taxes

Social: Health, Education, Fashion, Lifestyle, Migration, Population

Technical: Mobile, R&D, Data, Security, Internet, AI

Legal: Copyright, Employment, GDPR, Advertising, Consumer

Environmental: Climate, Recycling, Pollution, Waste, Renewables

EXERCISE

Have a look at the factors listed here under each heading and try to think of other factors which could have an indirect effect.

For example, the environment might force a situation that continues to raise taxes on air travel, which could have a detrimental impact if you rely on overseas trade.

The continued rise in manufacturing in China, might force raw materials shortages in the rest of the world, and so on.

Use the outcome from your PESTLE analysis to consider how the organisation will survive and prosper.

Introducing FurnFast

In March, the head of FurnFast (our fictitious organisation) announced that the Business Plan for the following year was to be put together over the next few weeks. It would, as usual, require additional management effort to get the plan finalised and approved before a meeting with the company owners in June.

Over the following weeks, the directors and managers worked together to formulate the plan. At the same time, each manager was asked to prepare a *departmental budget* for the coming year covering new equipment, staff, training, recruitment, materials, consumables, salaries, and bonuses.

Knowing they never received everything they requested, each manager budgeted for more than was required, hoping the directors would approve most of the projected expenditure.

The draft Business Plan document briefly summarised what had happened in the past 18 months regarding market demand, technology, imports, prices, and customers, with a summary of current market conditions and an outline of the plans for the coming year. The rest of the fifteen-page dossier contained financial projections of sales, overheads, expenditure, and profit, based upon the managers' *departmental budgets*.

The content of the plan was ratified at the monthly directors' meeting in June before being presented to the owners at a meeting one week later.

Back at the FurnFast Head Office, the plan was copied and circulated to directors, and an edited version (minus some of the financial projections) was copied and distributed to the managers.

Each of the recipients read it, filed it away securely, and there it stayed.

This charade, or something similar, is re-enacted in millions of organisations annually.

For FurnFast, the business planning activity was complete for yet another year, and no-one had seen the futility of the whole *process*.

The organisation had, again, failed to plan (or planned to fail).

Shortly after the Business Plan had been finalised and filed away, the managers learned the company owners had decided the entire organisation was going from a 12-hour-day to a 24-hour-day operation (with no concern for the additional costs).

Despite this significant decision, the Business Plan wasn't updated or reviewed. By neglecting to develop and utilise the plan, the organisation was failing to plan AND planning to fail.

FurnFast made some minor gains in sales, stock reduction and waste; they were happy with the modest growth at first. However, the competition continued to grow at a faster rate, which led to lower prices of imported competitive goods.

The situation gradually became critical, and drastic steps were required. The head of FurnFast finally realised it was time to revolutionise the organisation.

We're going to use FurnFast again later in this book as an example of some of the critical aspects of managing effective change.

Organisation

Occasionally, it's beneficial to go back to basics and review the organisational structure, and especially to define who's responsible for some of the minor processes and activities such as, security, cleaning, catering, window cleaning, server maintenance, or vending machine filling. From the review, it is possible to define the organisation across all activities, to identify individuals, and the chain of command, throughout the organisation.

The organisational review might uncover:

- Processes with no owner
- People with no supervisor
- Considerable wastage/duplication of effort
- A lack of understanding of the organisation, at all levels
- Conflicts between departments

The organisation structure review is an essential step in preparing for change – be thorough in the study, leave no stone unturned.

Be prepared for some surprises.

Review:
We covered many topics in Section 2:

- Business planning is the most crucial activity undertaken by an organisation.

- Having a first-rate Business Plan is not enough. The plan must then be communicated to everyone using terminology they understand.

- By cascading the objective and gradually translating it into tasks, it is then possible to identify the individuals who will be responsible for undertaking those tasks.

- Everyone has a unique role in the organisation – each needs a unique set of tasks to complete.

- Poor implementation is deemed to be the leading cause of failure. Poor implementation is a direct result of poor planning.

- 'The Business Plan was distributed to the managers. Each of them read it, filed it away securely, and there it stayed.' This charade, or something similar, is re-enacted in millions of organisations annually.

Section Three

Operational Tools and Controls

Definitions: *Operational - ready for proper use*
Tool - anything used to complete a task
Controls - a set of directions and checks

What to Expect

As the Business Plan is being developed and the tasks are being agreed, there will be heightened awareness within the organisation.

People will be talking more about their work; they will be enthused by their involvement in the implementation of the plan.

From this, organisations can expect:

Change; hardly surprising since that's what we're aiming for, but often the changes come rapidly; faster than anyone imagined. Aim for quick wins; get individuals accustomed to the changes, and more changes will come. Change promotes change.

Create a problem which has to be solved by the objective, for example, "Competition is fierce, raw material prices are increasing, and customers want more". Organisations and individuals often respond more effectively to real problems than initiatives aimed at *just being better.*

Improvement; the plan must ensure all changes are improvements – don't aim for significant improvements, aim for small gains on a consistent on-going basis. Plan and expect improvements in product/service quality and productivity; additional enhancements will follow, such as customer satisfaction, and employee morale.

Lots of Training; the Business Plan will highlight a need for training by specifying what will be expected from individuals across the organisation. Individuals must be encouraged to train in the first instance.

Under no circumstances must the need for training be seen as a weakness. Nobody knows everything.

It may be beneficial to provide small incentives to trainees: a pen, a writing pad, or a free lunch.

A good training regime, once established, will begin to snowball.

Individuals rarely want additional on-the-job training; they know how to do their work; what individuals want is to learn new skills to help them develop and equip them for promotion. Often the required training is more about soft skills, such as leadership, motivation, briefings, and communication.

Dissent; unfortunately, not everyone will get on board from the outset. Plan the launch of the campaign where the head of the organisation contacts every individual. In my experience, it's best to do this informally in small groups. Otherwise, the workers may feel intimidated.

Explain to everyone the reasons why the organisation is to undertake an incredible journey, where significant changes are going to be made, and the organisation is going to be better and stronger as a result.

All individuals will be involved in the changes, but they shouldn't be made to feel at risk or threatened – encourage everyone to get involved. Offer appropriate incentives to get individuals listening and thinking.

Don't go into detail during the launch; leave that aspect to the directors, the managers, and the supervisors, who will talk to the workers about the activities and tasks.

Management should ensure employees at every level understand the tasks so they can agree and commit to the changes. If individuals continue to oppose the Business Plan, management must tackle the problem as a matter of priority; get to the root of the dilemma.

Why should someone not want to see improvements?

Maybe people don't understand, or perhaps people feel threatened. Get everyone personally involved in the cascading process.

Enthusiasm; some individuals become motivated at the prospect of working on a project and being able to demonstrate their abilities.

Management should encourage involvement and get individuals enthused about the future, their organisation, and their career.

However, don't let over-enthusiasm lead to mistakes or shortcuts to get tasks completed.

Follow the plan.

Reduced Operating Costs; this is an intrinsic part of every Business Plan. Whatever the circumstance, reducing operating costs must be part of the plan, if only to finance the additional expenditure required to realise the objective. Aim to do things correctly, even if it costs money; short-term investments equal long-term savings.

Reduced Lead Times; in any organisation, it is possible to reduce the amount of time it takes to get anything done. Management should take a step back and assess areas in the organisation where products, individuals, and information are not moving.

As part of the new way of doing things, the organisation must reduce the lead times, look at alternative methods, streamline the processes, and remove the waiting time. Attempt to cut the lead times in every process, and not just those aspects of the organisation which relate to manufacturing or engineering. Specifically, avoid any needless delays in elements of the Business Plan, delays could be due to weak management commitment, which may cause frustration for individuals who are motivated and eager to make the changes.

Increased profits; if the expenditure is controlled and within established budgets, the reduced operating costs will begin to manifest as an increase in profits; this is not an accident.

If the entire organisation understands the objective and is working on the defined tasks, the objective will be achieved.

Improved communication; individuals will start to talk to each other and, what's more, they will begin to understand each other and the factors affecting their area of activity.

Individuals will discuss the problems, issues, worries, grievances, and concerns.

As a result, solutions will be found before they become significant issues; individuals often agree on courses of action because they're involved in the problem-solving.

Reports will soon become standardised across the organisation and will be published on a more frequent basis. Individuals will know what's going on; they will no longer be kept in the dark.

Breaches of confidentiality; I'm not suggesting, for one moment, that someone is going to steal the objective and sell it to the organisation's competitors. Management must be mindful of the content of the Business Plan – it sets out what the organisation is going to do to beat the competition.

Develop a communication plan which will tell the management *who knows what* within the organisation. The overall objective doesn't mean a lot to the majority of the individuals, but the added detail in the Business Plan makes it a precious document. Share only the pertinent points with individuals.

> "Successful teams have one mind but many thoughts."

Sense of Urgency

By building a sense of urgency, I'm not implying that organisations fast-track the development or the implementation of the Business Plan. Nor am I suggesting management cuts corners to get to the end of the project sooner. Rushing will cause failure; aim to complete the defined tasks as planned.

What I am suggesting is that management creates a sense of urgency in the early stages, to get the project started. Keep individuals buoyant and keep the project on track by following the plan and avoiding ANY delay.

At the outset, aim for easy short-term wins to get everyone motivated – success is a great motivator.

A statement from management, or the head of the organisation, if well-worded, will create the required motivation initially.

Unfortunately, I've seen organisations announce exciting projects which get everyone motivated, but then stall the launch for many weeks.

Individuals often forget the initial announcement and become confused when they begin to notice the changes.

Revolutionise

Many individuals are fearful of the term *revolution* when applied to their organisation. It infers a massive shake-up, a loss of control, and a venture into unexplored areas.

Here's the reality; if management doesn't revolutionise the organisation proactively, they may have to do it reactively to overcome a severe threat from competitors.

Competitors are revolutionising their organisations to get more customers; your customers. Management has to change the organisation, maintain the customer base, and increase the sales revenue.

It's not a *walk in the park*, and it won't happen overnight, but it does require a revolutionary approach.

Consider:

- Is your organisation willing to accept incremental, organic growth, which is mainly achieved through momentum, occasionally reacting to market forces to *stay in the game*?

Or

- Is your organisation ready to develop a revolutionary strategy for the radical change which seriously threatens the competitors and becomes embedded into every level of the organisation through a meticulously planned cascading process?

Do you want to be threatened or threatening? You choose!

A well-respected CEO once challenged me when I suggested he should revolutionise his organisation.

He acknowledged that the market was reaching its saturation point, his company was losing market share, some of the recent market entrants were lowering prices, material prices continued to rise, new Regulations adding complexity and cost, environmental pressures were looming, and profits were being hammered.

I simply suggested he should look at revolutionising his organisation, and he asked me why when his organisation was doing OK, better than most.

"*For all the reasons you've just given me,*" I replied.

"*Look, I'm busy; I don't need this.*" was his response.

"*What, you don't need to change what you're doing? Of course, you do.*" I managed to impart before he terminated the phone call.

This is a true story.

Less than six months later, I was hired to assess and purchase whatever parts of the failed business were worth buying; I came away with nothing.

The organisation, which had once been a market leader, collapsed spectacularly because the owner believed evolution would ensure continued success. He knew the market pressures but was unwilling to deal with them.

Yesterday's successes won't satisfy the customers of tomorrow

Project Approval Status

Although organisations plan for a smooth change, there will be a need to modify some of the project tasks as they're being implemented. It isn't possible to develop a Business Plan which can exist for more than a few weeks without the need to amend it. So, although the plan may be approved, it could be subjected to frequent changes, which will also need to be accepted.

It is essential that any approved changes are incorporated into the Business Plan immediately, and the amendments are published to everyone who is affected by the change.

The approval of any modifications to the Business Plan should be swift; delays could stifle the organisational development and the enthusiasm of individuals and prevent them from completing their assigned tasks.

Expenditure

In many large projects, the approval of the plan infers the adoption of any associated costs, including recruitment.

However, with a project of this size and nature, there is a need to control the tasks which require expenditure and resource.

The Business Plan should require expenditure and recruitment to be controlled by proper authorisation.

Proper authorisation is the processes which are usually used to control expenditure and recruitment in the organisation.

Management may find, in some cases, the existing authorisation processes are threatening to slow the progress of the project. Organisations should review those processes, and the levels of authorisation, to reduce delays or bottlenecks.

I recommend, especially in the early stages of the project, short management meetings are held regularly to approve the necessary expenditure and recruitment. The short meetings keep the project moving and allow the finances to be controlled and approved accordingly. It is important to have the financial controls in place, but those controls should not cause the project to fail.

It may be appropriate to review each of the existing processes and controls which relate to Project Management and to determine their on-going suitability for the new project.

Organisations may find management delays have a significant effect on the project; this will cause frustration initially, which tends to develop into a lack of priority, and then the project starts to fail.

Meetings

Meetings are an essential management tool, especially for a massive multi-disciplinary project. In my experience, during the period of change, it is useful to hold dedicated meetings to discuss the Business Plan and its implementation.

It is important for Management to establish unambiguous ground rules for meetings. Those rules should cover the timing of meetings, the length of meetings, attendance, reporting, and subject matter.

Every session should have a purpose and a defined outcome.

Meetings are held almost continuously in every organisation in the world, but I still find many meetings are not controlled, do not stick to the subject and, as a result, are ineffective.

Training is often required for the people who are arranging, attending and reporting meetings. Such training pays dividends very quickly.

The golden rule for any meeting, *do not save important issues until the meeting*, tackle those problems as part of the day-to-day operation. Managers should report to each other directly instead of waiting for the next scheduled meeting.

Photograph Four: Bad meeting

Many years ago, towards the end of a very long meeting with my Group Chairman, the attendees were informed of a problem; something that I probably should have dealt with (had I known about it).

I asked the messenger how long he'd known about the issue.

"About three weeks".

So, why hadn't he told anyone? With a smug look on his face, he was merely waiting to see the reaction of the Chairman. Fortunately, the Chairman saw the politics as it played-out and had a *quiet word* with the offender.

The issue cost the organisation thousands of pounds but could have been resolved very quickly and cheaply had timely action been taken.

Recruitment

Remember the good old days when individuals often got recruited because they knew someone in the office?

Business is more onerous now, and it's going to get tougher still.

Recruitment of individuals can be a big issue when an organisation is undertaking a significant change. Identifying the future role of new recruits is essential.

Tougher business requires only the ideal candidates get into the organisation, i.e. those individuals with excellent qualifications and a good track record.

This approach should encourage management to review the organisation's recruitment policy and processes, ensuring that the processes don't become a barrier to appointing the necessary resources across the organisation.

Tools

I've mentioned that I'm unforgiving when it comes to management ability.

Anyone working in a management position, or higher, should have the necessary management skills and should be able to use management tools appropriately and efficiently. A poor manager can destroy an organisation.

To control the use of management tools, and to ensure the tools are being used correctly, the organisation should define which methods should be utilised and then offer to train all who need to use them.

Brainstorming

Brainstorming is a useful management tool mainly when problems need to be discussed and solved; it allows free-thinking and often generates seemingly wild ideas which can develop into something useful.

Individuals can brainstorm on their own, but this severely limits the scope of the ideas.

Brainstorming in teams, on the other hand, produces a more abundant array of suggestions, because the team members can adapt the opinions voiced by other team members.

To be successful, brainstorming requires the problem to be accurately described; it is a common mistake to make. Ensure the problem is clearly documented and understood before the brainstorming begins; otherwise, the exercise won't solve the problem.

Ideally, each team member should be able to share ideas freely, with no discussion or criticism.

The Chair of the session should encourage all individuals to participate.

All ideas must be recorded, preferably on small pieces of card or sticky notes. Similar or linking ideas can then be grouped together during the review period.

The most significant advantage of brainstorming is that it ensures everyone is conversant with the problem under discussion and can contribute to finding a solution.

Brainstorming is not a complicated or lengthy process and can be used to get a quick agreement on the resolution.

Failure Mode Effect Analysis (FMEA)

FMEA is the most useful tool for improvement; it is a systematic approach to the assessment of products and processes. FMEA provides an opportunity for organisations to foresee problems at an early stage in the product or process development programme, i.e. before design, development and launch.

FMEA allows the organisation to assess the effect of potential failures, according to:

- the severity of the effect,
- the probability of the occurrence, and
- the detectability of the failure.

It is essential for users to understand how to conduct an FMEA correctly. FMEA output is worthless if the inputs and the analysis are not complete and robust.

In this respect, training and guidance are often required to ensure completeness and accuracy.

FMEA Number:	FMEA Prepared by:	FMEA Date:
Product/Process Name:	FMEA Core Team:	
Product/Process Owner:	New or Current Product/Process?	Date for Review:

ANALYSIS							ACTION RESULTS			
Characteristic Name	Potential Failure Mode	Potential Effects of Failure	Severity (S)	Potential Causes of Failure	Probability (P)	Detection (D)	RPN (SxPxD)	Required Actions	Actions Taken	S	P	D	RPN

Illustration Two: FMEA chart

FMEA is often seen to be a time-consuming and expensive exercise, however:

- It identifies the root causes of potential failures,
- It allows the development of preventive actions BEFORE the failure occurs,
- It identifies the safety-critical characteristics of products and processes,
- It determines the safety and the longevity aspects of a product or process,
- It reduces the risk of failure, the effect of failure, and the cost of failure.

Service Level Agreements (SLAs)

SLAs are an easy way of making mutual arrangements for the delivery of tasks in the Business Plan. Teamwork is required to deliver the objective; using the efforts of cross-functional teams, some of the tasks will be easier to achieve. Those teams don't need to have a formal structure; they can be a group of individuals with a joint mission.

Simple agreements to work together, and to provide timely information and support to each other, can foster teamwork and the practical completion of the scheduled tasks.

Simple SLA: This SLA is contingent upon [team name] and [team name] knowing and fulfilling their responsibilities for the achievement of stated service levels:

1. Responding to all requests for information in accordance with the project plan.

2. Communicating any concerns over the timescales in the project plan.

3. Updating the project plan each week.

With simple SLAs, the team members promise to consider the priorities and workload of their team members and provide the necessary, timely support to achieve the task.

Project Facilitator

Undertaking significant change will lead the organisation into unfamiliar territory; the organisation has never been there before. At the end of the project, products and processes may be different as might the customers, the suppliers, the equipment, and so on.

No individuals inside the organisation have the skill, experience, or time, to manage all the changes on their own. In that respect, the organisational structure should be used to deliver the changes. The existing structure can achieve the tasks and objective using the cascading process.

However, the changes need to be overseen and monitored by an individual, or team of individuals, depending on the size and complexity of the organisation. The role of the project facilitator should be assigned to a manager who has an excellent overview of the organisation and can communicate effectively at all levels.

The function of the project facilitator is to monitor and report the project progress and to remove any barriers, hurdles and bottlenecks.

The facilitator should be available to provide practical hands-on support and training on Problem Solving, for example, to individuals and teams.

The facilitator should be able to operate freely throughout the organisation, at any level, providing guidance, support and feedback.

Outside Support and Expertise

If the organisation is not comfortable taking the first steps to develop a strategy and managing the changes, then find someone who is; don't avoid making the changes just because management has no experience of developing strategies and plans.

Likewise, it may be beneficial to seek professional support to help to guide the various meetings towards their objectives, targets, goals, and tasks. Someone with expertise in this field could bring much-needed guidance, an impartial view, and the ability to coordinate the efforts.

Take time to get it right–don't rush headlong into something unless you feel comfortable that it's going to work. Minor inconsistencies can be tackled as the project progresses, but serious concerns have to be carefully considered, and overcome, before the Business Plan can be finalised.

Management and individuals obviously understand the organisation, the processes, the business and the industry. However, the management of change is often something new; no-one in the organisation will have done this before.

Seeking the support of a management consultant with knowledge and experience can pay dividends. They can guide the project from the outset, getting it defined and planned, and supporting the communication, the cascading, and the monitoring.

Celebration

It is vital for the organisation to acknowledge that someone (or maybe everyone) has done something positive, recognising the efforts of individuals and teams in completing their tasks. Appreciation should relate to what the individual or team has achieved.

Personalise the recognition; simple things are often most productive; time off, a personal letter, a mention in the monthly newsletter/meeting/briefing, a photograph on the notice board.

Compensation should take many forms – money is not the only option – and can be a short-term reward. Set compensation rules whereby real effort and achievement should be rewarded according to the individual and the size of the gains. However, don't attempt to formalise the reward structure too strictly, or it will become an administrative burden. Compensate individuals and teams by what they deserve; try to be fair and consistent, and not show favouritism.

I was involved in a Suggestion Scheme in an organisation where individuals had to make suggestions and justify the size of their award by writing to a committee which judged excellent performance. The committee, comprising senior managers, met once a month for a full day.

Each application took many months to discuss and process, and the rewards (which were publicised) were always considered to be unfair (either too large or too small) and totally inconsistent. The suggestion scheme frustrated employees, but many were keen to make suggestions and see if they got lucky.

Top management believed the scheme was beneficial to employees but not to the organisation and realised the scheme was incredibly expensive to maintain.

I was asked to get involved to see if the scheme could be improved. Easy; I told the organisation to scrap the scheme and pay the awards as a performance bonus. Managers encouraged the workforce to contribute to the improvement of performance for the benefit of the organisation, with discretionary awards, and performance-related bonus payments.

So, as well as awarding individuals, it is possible to award teams or the entire workforce.

I know of cases where this has worked well. However, in some situations, it can cause in-fighting, especially where some teams don't realise what other groups are contributing. This a communication problem; all success should be communicated before it is rewarded. Management must announce the success before making the award.

Incentives could include:

Free meals
Free gym membership
Incentive travel
Working from home
Bonus scheme
Profit share
Share allocation
Healthcare
Dental care
Childcare
Party
Gift

Alternatively, the directors could simply say thank you.

Photograph Five: Thank you!

Review:

Section 3 introduced many new topics:

- If necessary, create a problem to be solved by the objective. Organisations and individuals often respond to real problems than those initiatives aimed at *just being better.*

- Individuals shouldn't be made to feel at risk or threatened – encourage everyone to get involved.

- A statement from the head of the organisation, if well-worded, will create the required motivation initially.

- Competitors are revolutionising their organisations to get your customers.

- Don't save essential issues until the next meeting; tackle those problems as part of the day-to-day operation.

Section Four

Making the Changes

Definitions: *Make - to bring about*
Change - to make something different

The final section of the book deals with making the changes by putting everything we've learned into use.

In the previous sections, we looked at Route Plans, the content of Business Plans and Prime Objectives. So, how do we start putting all of this together?

The Baseline

In the introduction, I stated that the baseline is the starting point for all future performance trends, so that's where we start; by determining where the organisation is now.

Actually, it's not as easy as it sounds (unless the organisation has effective KPIs in place).

The directors must decide what's important to the organisation and what needs to be measured. The number of stock lines (large or small), the speed of delivery, the number of lost-time-accidents (zero, hopefully), the number of customers, the percentage market share, and so on.

It seems the head of FurnFast (our fictitious organisation) has an issue with customers placing small orders; they increase internal costs arising from order processing and invoicing, etc. The head issued an instruction to the salesforce to encourage (incentivise) customers to place larger orders. It seems the instruction has been largely ignored.

FurnFast's current position – the baseline – is defined as:

Sales revenue per week	£1,148,400
Number of employees	575
Cost per employee per week	£526
Revenue per employee per week	£1,997
Number of customers	251
Number of orders per week	840
Number of orders per customer per week	3.35
Order value	£1,374
Number of components sold per week	2,000,000

As the Business Plan is being developed, the organisation will identify other baseline measures which must be added to the list.

Try not to get too many baseline measures; aim for a maximum of 12. Also, don't go into too much detail.

By establishing and agreeing on the baseline, the directors will be able to see the net effect of any planned changes, and also understand – from the outset – the size of the tasks in front of them.

It's important for the baseline calculations to be accurate, true, and fully understood by the directors and managers. Some crucial decisions are going to made using these figures.

The head of the organisation might, for example, be pushing for increased revenue (say 10%) without increasing the number of employees.

However, what if the baseline figures are inaccurate or false? Any change in the performance would go unnoticed, to the detriment of the organisation.

I recall a meeting where the head of finance blurted out,

"We should increase all prices immediately; clearly there is a demand for product x so we should see if a 10% increase makes a difference to sales."

"Interesting statement," I replied, "what is the current price of 'product x'?"

"Well, I don't know exactly. I suppose it's around one thousand pounds. Taking it to eleven hundred pounds won't affect the uptake."

"It's one thousand, four hundred and forty pounds."

The head of finance – totally embarrassed – didn't know where to look.

The price was the highest in the market, for a product which wasn't unique. Everyone in the room now realised the company couldn't afford to raise the price. The product was being sold at a premium.

More importantly, the Board avoided making a bad decision based on misinformation – get the facts right.

The Directors

The FurnFast Directors are:

- Managing Director (the head)
- Financial Director
- Technical Director
- Sales Director
- Operations Director
- Logistics Director
- HR Director

Let's have a look at the detail of the cascading process. The cascade translates the prime objective into something which is understandable to the organisation. The most effective way to start the cascade process is to present the objective to the directors and let them have their say in the future of the organisation. I use the term directors, by which I mean the most senior members of the organisation – see the FurnFast Organisation Profile in ANNEX 1.

Giving the directors an opportunity to discuss the Prime Objective also ensures they understand and agree with the objective and are able to demonstrate their commitment to realising it.

This is the first stage in cascading the objective through the organisation. Get this process wrong, and the rest will fail.

Plan a Prime Objective meeting, allowing plenty of time to get through the workload. I would suggest this initial meeting might last, at least, one day. In my experience, this meeting should be held off-site in a neutral location to facilitate full and frank discussion. Ensure all the directors are involved in this meeting. 100% attendance, no less.

The Prime Objective Meeting marks the start of the revolution, and so if a director is unable to attend it, reschedule the meeting. Do not, under any circumstances, leave anyone behind.

The meeting agenda might look something like this:

- Item 1   Organisation performance (the baseline)
- Item 2   Market performance
- Item 3   Organisation projections
- Item 4   Market outlook
- Item 5   Vision: Where do we want to be?
- Item 6   Formulation of the Prime Objective
    - Is the Prime Objective SMART?
    - Overall Timescales
    - Individual Responsibilities
- Item 7   The Strategy

The meeting should start by presenting an overview of the organisation and market performance, and the outlook for both. The head should present a vision (where do we want to be?) of the future of the organisation, with justification in the form of market threats, business risks, and opportunities.

When delivering the presentation, consider the audience and direct the content to them as individuals so they may identify with the vision.

With the full commitment of each of the directors, they need to translate the vision into something which defines what the organisation aims to achieve – the Prime Objective. The Prime Objective quantifies the vision and makes it easier to convert the vision into actions at all levels in the organisation.

By adding detail to the Prime Objective at the highest level, it becomes The Strategy describing what the organisation is going to do and outlining how the organisation is going to do it.

At each successive level in the organisation, more detail is added to describe precisely how the organisation will achieve the Prime Objective.

That's the key; don't expect everyone in the organisation to understand the Prime Objective.

However, by cascading the objective through the organisation structure, it gets translated at each level into something which is understandable.

Do you remember the hierarchy structure from the Introduction?

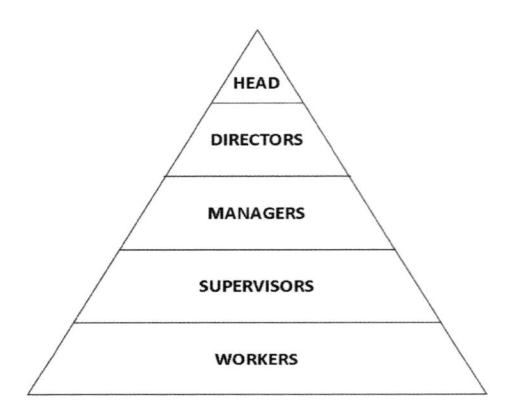

```
        /\
       /HEAD\
      /------\
     /DIRECTORS\
    /------------\
   /  MANAGERS    \
  /----------------\
 /   SUPERVISORS    \
/--------------------\
/      WORKERS        \
------------------------
```

This structure is the reporting structure; the levels do not relate to salary bands or job titles.

The structure is similar to the cascading structure (Figure Seven), which shows how the various targets, activities and tasks get translated, understood, and agreed at each level, with the full participation of everyone at the same level.

The head of the organisation is responsible for creating the vision and, with the support of the directors, develop the Prime Objective. The directors support the head in developing the Prime Objective and, with the support of the managers, develop The Strategy.

Each level in the organisation is responsible for translating and communicating the details through the cascading structure.

This approach ensures understanding, agreement and commitment throughout the organisation.

The Prime Objective

There's no magic formula for developing a Prime Objective, but the resultant statement should reinforce the vision, and add sufficient detail to specify what's going to be done, and when it's going to be done by.

The wording has to be unambiguous, and it must appeal to everyone connected with the organisation at every level – individuals, suppliers, stakeholders, customers, and visitors.

For example, suppose the vision is:

"To be the market leader, and begin to branch out into new markets."

Okay, so it's not perfect, but it's a start. We now need to add detail and clarity:

- What are we to be the market leader of?
- When are we going to be the market leader?
- What new markets are we considering?
- How much income might we expect from those new markets?
- When can we expect the new markets to bring new income?

At the director and management level, the Prime Objective must be FULLY understood and agreed prior to it being published. Each director and manager must be FULLY committed to making it happen.

It usually takes several attempts to perfect the wording and the meaning of the Prime Objective.

It's good practice to explain the objective, by adding clarification.

For example,

"To become the market leader in the supply of spring-fastening products to the UK furniture industry, and to diversify into complimentary markets and products, which should account for an additional 10% of sales revenue, in 2025."

Alternatively,

"As Europe's market leader in the widget industry, in 2025, FurnFast will have a profitable sales revenue in excess of £120m, an increase of £60m (100%) on current sales."

These statements could be fine-tuned to read:

"To be Europe's leading manufacturer and supplier of furniture widgets with profitable annual income in excess of £120 million in 2025.

Within the same period, FurnFast will diversify into complementary markets and products, which should account for over 10% of the new sales revenue."

For guidance, consider using this template as a starting point:

"To be a leading [organisation type] of [product/service] with [target] by [when]. Delivering the most [description] [products or services] to [customers]."

By filling in the blanks, the Prime Objective might say something like this:

"To be a leading UK provider of home contents insurance, with profitable income of £250 million annually by delivering 45% growth by 2024."

Alternatively, the Prime Objective could relate to profitability:

"To achieve a 25% return on capital employed by August 2025".

Equally, it could be market share related:

"To gain 25% of the UK market for sports shoes by August 2025."

Remember, there's no need to rush this; it is essential to make sure the directors fully understand the Prime Objective and are totally committed to achieving it.

We may need a few words to add further clarity as to what this means for the organisation:

"The European market leader in our industry, in 2025, will have profitable sales revenues in excess of £120m per annum, an increase of over £60m (100%) on current sales revenue.

Over £12m of profitable sales-revenue per annum, in 2025, will come from new markets and/or products.

Therefore, sales revenue has to be increased by £60m (100%) by 2025."

The Prime Objective should specify what must be done and not how it will be done.

The strategy will begin to describe how the Prime Objective will be achieved.

So, now we have a Prime Objective, and we're keen to tell everyone. However, a note of caution; confidentiality is a crucial issue. We want the good guys to know what we're doing (our employees, suppliers, stakeholders, customers, and visitors), but we don't want the bad guys to know (our competitors).

Since the Prime Objective sets out what you're going to do to beat the competition, communicate the Prime Objective carefully – it's advisable to develop a communication plan so you can control the dissipation of various levels of objectives, goals, and targets, plus you will be aware of *who knows what* within the organisation.

In its present form, the Prime Objective will mean very little to the majority of the workers, so that's what we're going to do next. We're going to start to translate the Prime Objective into something everyone can begin to understand.

Taking the example shown, each director, working with the other directors, determines how the Prime Objective will be achieved; the output from the directors will form the strategy.

With an agreed strategy in place, each director works with their managers to define how the strategy will be achieved.

Explaining the strategy to the managers gains a high level of understanding and commitment. The output from the managers will be a set of goals.

Each manager then goes to their supervisors and determines how each goal will be realised.

Each supervisor must show a high level of understanding of the goals and a commitment to achieving them.

Each supervisor then goes to the workers and discusses the goals, seeking valuable input from the worker and gaining a commitment to the objective.

The output of the discussion is a set of tasks to be completed by the workers.

At the point where the workers are involved in defining tasks, the Prime Objective has been cascaded into the organisation.

Strategy

The Prime Objective is a global statement, so we need to break it down into manageable chunks and begin to address how we're going to generate an additional 100% of profitable sales.

It's too easy for each of the directors to scurry off into their departments and begin to do something. However, at this stage, any urge to *get on with it* must be resisted – we're still in the planning stage.

It's time for another meeting; this time we're going to discuss what the organisation is going to do to achieve the Prime Objective.

There is only one agenda item:

- Item 1: How will we achieve the Prime Objective?

Since the directors are familiar with the Prime Objective, and have made a commitment to delivering it, each should be fully prepared to come to the meeting with proposals outlining what can be done in their area of responsibility to fulfil the Prime Objective. Additionally, each director should have discussed their proposals with each of the other directors.

Each director should also have started the cascading process by informing their managers. The managers should now be aware of the Prime Objective, they should fully understand it, and should have made a firm commitment to achieving it.

I would expect a director-level strategy meeting to last for one full day. There's a lot to get through, and this process is new to every one of the attendees. Again, aim for 100% attendance – all directors must give this meeting their full attention.

The strategy meeting is critical to the realisation of the vision and the achievement of the Prime Objective. Organisations only get one shot at this; they can't afford to mess it up.

The meeting should start with the head reminding the directors of the vision and the prime objective.

"As the European market leader in our industry, in 2025, FurnFast will have profitable sales revenues in excess of £120m per annum, an increase of over £60m (100%) on current sales revenue.

Over £12m of profitable sales-revenue, in 2025, will come from new markets and/or products.

Therefore, sales revenue has to be increased by £60m (100%) by 2025."

Each director, having done their homework, should then present their proposals to achieve the Prime Objective; again, we're not looking for a lot of detail, we're just adding clarity. The timeframe is already set, and the growth rate has been specified. So, what is the organisation going to do to achieve the Prime Objective?

It's important to discuss each proposal as it's presented to ensure it's fully understood, and it fits in the overall plan.

From the PESTLE analysis, let's assume the following were highlighted, for example:

- Trade will become tougher as imports from China continue to flood the market.
- Prices will continue to fall for the next year, at least.
- However, Chinese suppliers will not be able to provide a full service to European customers.
- Inflation will continue to rise modestly, and interest rates will remain stable.
- Exchange rates will tighten before easing in 2-3 years.
- Immigration will slow, making it difficult to find manual workers.
- Recycling will continue to drive environmental efforts against a backdrop of taxes and tariffs.

The first decision the FurnFast directors have to consider is whether there was a long-term future in the present market and the organisation.

At this stage, most organisations realise that they have to change significantly to be able to secure new business, increase revenues and maintain profitability, for example.

At FurnFast, as the discussions around the individual proposals were developing, it was clear the organisation needed to invest to survive. The head committed to any investment that would secure the long-term future but warned that the investment had to be low-risk and there wasn't an endless fund.

In the initial strategy meetings, I find the best approach is to seek input from each director in the form of a short presentation on how they propose to meet the prime objective in their department. Each can be discussed, adjusted and agreed.

At the first FurnFast strategy meeting, the directors agreed to:

Financial

Develop new pricing and discount strategies tailored to each customer. These would be based on the margins for each product, the volumes being purchased, the number of orders (and the order size), the ease of delivery, and the level of technical support required by the customer.

With some customers running credit lines of up to 90 days, the meeting agreed to incentivise an early payment scheme, with additional discounts for payment with order.

The Finance Director suggested that each department should review and reduce all costs across all activities, with a target of 10%. The meeting agreed that this should not be seen as a staff reduction exercise.

During the meeting, the directors recognised that they didn't have access to pertinent data and agreed to improve the availability and accuracy of management information.

Technical

A technical review of competitor products revealed that, by comparison of weight, the FurnFast products were heavier and more expensive.

The Technical Director proposed to redesign the products to reduce the weight, which will lower the material cost, the shipping cost and, with careful design, could reduce the waste levels.

The directors recognised the need for significant investment, but initial estimates showed the investment would be recovered within weeks.

In the discussions over the limited offerings from Chinese competitors, the meeting realised that most couldn't provide a full service due to logistics.

The proposal was to assess a range of complementary products to sell to the existing customers, e.g. hand tools, etc.

Arising from the discussion on hand tools and the application or fitting of the products, the meeting agreed to innovate the product designs specifically for ease of application by the customer. Making the customers' process more effective would be a key USP.

Sales

The Sales Director proposed to launch a major marketing campaign to drive sales and new customers and to promote the new products.

There was a long discussion about lowering prices across the range to encourage new business and reduce the risk of losing existing customers. This would be on a customer by customer basis, and most would be achieved through discounts and incentives.

The meeting agreed to assess alternative markets for the same range of products. The focus on furniture was perhaps too narrow.

Operations

The meeting agreed to invest in new tooling and equipment to gradually increase output to meet rising customer demands.

The product redesign would be coordinated with the operational team to improve productivity.

The Operations Director proposed to increase efficiencies by raising the output and reducing the wastage and downtime.

The head of FurnFast warned about the need to balance output and demand; any misalignment would lead to overstocking or failing to supply.

The basic calculations showed that the organisation had to increase production output by over 100% over the period, depending on the achieved savings and discounts to customers.

However, by agreeing to purchase and factor more components and sub-assemblies from China, the manufacturing output would need to increase by just under 100%.

Logistics

To maximise the use of vehicle load space, the meeting agreed to encourage bulk deliveries by offering additional discounts.

The Logistics Director noted that bulk deliveries might require the use of alternative lifting and storage equipment.

As part of the increase in manufacturing output, the meeting had already agreed to purchase factored components and sub-assemblies from Chinese suppliers to reduce the cost.

Achieving 100% stock accuracy was considered a critical factor in maintaining supplies to customers.

Human Resources

Having identified that the Chinese competitors couldn't provide customer service, the directors agreed to develop a bespoke customer service team to provide seamless support to customers.

The customer service team would ensure that the products were being integrated into the customers' products and processes effectively and efficiently.

The team would provide all required training.

Overall

To be the market leader, the directors agreed to further improve the quality of all products and services internally and externally.

To deliver initiatives, projects, products and services, the meeting decided that the organisation should aim to achieve 100% schedule adherence across all activities.

Additionally, increased throughput and activity can lead to an increased rate of mistakes and accidents.

The directors committed to reducing the number and severity of Lost Time Accidents (LTAs).

As for the "***Over £12m of profitable sales-revenue per annum, in 2025, will come from new markets and/or products.***", the meeting agreed not to ignore any opportunities for developing new products for new markets. However, it decided to concentrate on developing new products for existing markets, and then look to sell those products into new markets.

Some of these Strategic Goals are not very specific, but it's not a problem at this stage – it gives the organisation something to discuss and agree at the next steps.

What we have to do now is to begin to collate the Prime Objective and the top-level goals into a single strategy, which we can then continue to develop into a project plan.

There's only one way of doing this correctly, and it's the key to the success or failure of the cascading process; develop a project plan for the organisation.

With a project plan, you can include the tasks, the resources, the timescales, and the dependencies. Plus, it can be very detailed – the more detail you include on the project plan, the more success you will have. A project plan can be easily monitored and amended.

This is when the Project Coordinator needs to get involved and begin to define the project. The prime objective and the top-level goals can be added to the project at this stage, but the required resources and specific timescales cannot be set until the strategy has been cascaded through the organisation and agreed.

I'm not going to get into the detail of project management here, but in a project plan, just like in reality, activities tend to rely upon each other, so it's not possible to specify the start and finish times of each task. The dependencies of one task to the next can be defined, but only when all the tasks have been collated can the organisation begin to consider the resources and timescales.

In many respects, the project plan is similar to a giant jigsaw puzzle, except we don't know what the picture is, and we don't know how many pieces there are. However, we do know we haven't yet got all of the parts.

As the strategy is cascaded into the organisation, the detail of the project plan is developed, level by level, until we've defined the tasks to be carried out by individuals, along with timescales for completion. These individuals can then see how their contribution is going to earn the organisation an additional £60m per year.

From this stage on, the head must support the directors and managers in the cascading process. The progress of the cascading will be reported on a regular basis, and meetings will be held to discuss any issues.

Once the project is launched, the reporting will be via the existing channels, with the added benefit of a live project plan.

The head of the organisation has two essential tasks they must complete. Both tasks are extremely useful at this early stage in the project.

The first task is to create a form of words, a statement, capturing the prime objective and the top-level goals from the strategy meeting.

The statement will be used across the entire organisation from suppliers to customers and, especially, the managers, supervisors and workers.

The statement might take some time to develop – it's often worth involving the marketing team to find the right words.

At all costs, do not release the statement until the head and the directors are in total agreement, for example:

Strategy for Success

FurnFast, the European market leader in the furniture components industry, will have profitable sales revenues in excess of £120m in 2025, an increase of over £60m (100%) on current sales revenue.

In 2025, over £12m of profitable sales-revenue will come from new markets and/or new products. FurnFast is committed to investing to secure the long-term future of the organisation.

To achieve the Prime Objective, the company is committed to:

- Developing new pricing and discount strategies tailored to each customer.
- Incentivising an early payment scheme, with discounts for payment with order.
- Reviewing and reducing all costs across all activities, with a target of 10%.
- Improving the availability and accuracy of management information.
- Redesigning products to lower the cost and reduce waste.
- Assessing a range of complementary products to sell to the existing customers, e.g. hand tools, etc.
- Innovating the product designs specifically for ease of application by the customer.

- Launching a marketing campaign to drive sales and new customers, and to promote the new products.
- Lowering prices across the range to encourage new business and reduce the risk of losing customers.
- Assessing alternative markets for the same range of products.
- Investing in new tooling and equipment to gradually increase output to meet rising customer demands.
- Increasing efficiencies by reducing wastage and downtime.
- Purchasing and factoring more components and sub-assemblies from China.
- Encouraging bulk deliveries by offering additional discounts.
- Achieving 100% stock accuracy.
- Developing a bespoke service team to provide seamless support to customers.
- Further improving the quality of all products and services internally and externally.
- Achieving 100% schedule adherence across all activities.
- Reducing the number and severity of Lost Time Accidents (LTAs).

This is our "**Strategy for Success**"; it defines the structure of our project plan.

The second task is to imagine FurnFast 2025 compared to FurnFast now:

	FurnFast now	FurnFast 2025
Sales revenue	£60m	£120m
Number of employees	575	695
Revenue per employee	£104,347	£173,000
Number of customers	251	550
Number of orders per week	840	580
Number of orders per customer	3.35	1.05
Average order value	£1,367	£3,960
Number of components sold per week	2,000,000	3,636,000

Table One: The crystal ball

In this example, the content of Table One is not realistic – it's just an example; however, it serves to show what the organisation might look like in a few years.

I encourage all organisations to create such a table and, whenever I see the numbers, I'm always pleasantly surprised to see the step-change in such a short period.

At this early stage, no-one needs to get over-concerned about the size of the project, or the details of the necessary improvements, concentrate upon the strategy itself, but be aware FurnFast could potentially make, pack, store, sell, and ship an additional 82 million products per year.

None of the big numbers should cause an organisation to alter its strategy. All of the aspects which need to be considered can be raised and discussed at the appropriate time.

The Project Plan will contain sufficient detail to allow the organisation to plan ahead and to consider the issues at the right time and the right level; so, there is no need to get bogged down in detail at this point.

Just because the sales revenue increases significantly over the period, that doesn't mean the number of individuals has to rise by the same proportion. Likewise, the number of customers and the number of customer orders don't need to increase in-line with the rise in sales revenue.

Realistically, the number of components probably does need to increase proportionately – unless the organisation thinks its customers would accept a price increase; I didn't see price increases mentioned in the strategy.

What Table One does, is to show there are many other issues to consider; and these should be allowed for in the cascading process.

The Cascading Organisation

We started with a vision. With the directors, we translated the vision into the Prime Objective. Then, with the directors, we fine-tuned the Prime Objective, added detail and converted it into The Strategy. The next stage is for the directors to cascade The Strategy down to the managers and, with their support, create the next level of detail – the management targets.

Those targets will be added to the project plan before being cascaded down to the supervisors and, with their support, create the next level of detail – the departmental goals, which are added to the project plan. The cascading process continues as the supervisors cascade the goals down to the workers and with their support, create the tasks, which are added to the project plan.

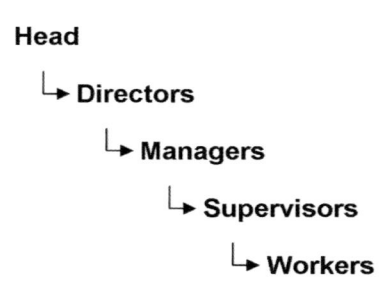

Head
　↳ **Directors**
　　↳ **Managers**
　　　↳ **Supervisors**
　　　　↳ **Workers**

This cascading structure demonstrates how the vision is converted into activity.

Cascading is not a one-stage process; far from it. At every level, in every activity, and with every individual, there must be a unique plan which is fully understood, agreed and committed-to.

The process of cascading and developing the Business Plan might take several weeks, or even months, depending upon the size of the organisation and the type of activity undertaken.

It is imperative that the strategy is FULLY understood and agreed, by the directors, before publication. Each director must demonstrate a total committed to achieving the strategy and the project plan developed from it. In this example, we show how the prime objective is cascaded.

The directors, working together, establish how each element of the prime objective will be achieved. The directors should demonstrate an understanding of the prime objective and show a commitment to delivering it.

Using the Prime Objective: FurnFast, the European market leader in the furniture components industry, will have profitable sales revenues in excess of £120m in 2025, an increase of over £60m (100%) on current sales revenue. In 2025, over £12m of profitable sales-revenue will come from new markets and/or new products.

The directors defined the strategy shown here. Each element of the strategy was added to the project plan.

The Prime Objective will be achieved by:

1.1 Developing new pricing and discount strategies tailored to each customer.

1.2 Redesigning products to lower the cost, and reduce waste

1.3 Innovating the product designs specifically for ease of application by the customer.

1.4 Launching a marketing campaign to drive sales and new customers and to promote the new products.

1.5 And so on.

Each director discussed the strategy with their managers and between them, after two or three meetings, determined how it would be achieved.

At this level, there wasn't a need to discuss the entire strategy, only those parts which affect their areas of responsibility.

Each manager must demonstrate a high level of understanding of the objective and a substantial commitment to achieving it.

Let's take one of the elements from the FurnFast strategy:

1.4   Launching a marketing campaign to drive sales and new customers and to promote the new products.

Using the same brainstorming and thought process the directors used to translate the Prime Objective into the strategy, the directors and managers will translate the strategy into management targets, one element at a time:

In the FurnFast sales department, for example, the Sales Director and Managers agreed to:

1.4.1   Create multimedia marketing material for use across the web, social media, and emails
1.4.2   Exhibit at all major exhibitions
1.4.3   Create a strong social media presence
1.4.4   Track, report and analyse all online and email metrics; building campaigns to boost traction
1.4.5   And so on

Notice how we've introduced a numbering system; this allows us to track the individual tasks and determine how they support the achievement of the strategy.

The numbering system also allows the tracking of the progress of the tasks in the project plan.

The same process of translation is then completed for each of the management targets. With 21 managers working for FurnFast, if each generates five targets, that's 105 management targets in total.

At each level, we just add more detail to describe how the prime objective will be achieved.

Let's take one of the management targets from the FurnFast sales department:

1.4.3   Create a strong social media presence

Again, by using the same brainstorming and thought process the directors and managers used to translate the strategy into management targets, the managers and supervisors will translate the management targets into departmental goals, one element at a time.

In the FurnFast sales department, for example, the Sales and Marketing Managers along with the Sales Executives and Coordinators agreed to:

1.4.3.1 Identify the social media audience and what platforms they might use

1.4.3.2 Select social media platforms to use

1.4.3.3 Develop processes to create great social media content

1.4.3.4 Engage followers by posting relevant content regularly

1.4.3.5 And so on.

The same process of translation is then completed for each of the departmental goals.

Assuming 105 management targets, if each translates to five departmental goals, that's 525 departmental goals in total.

In practice, there will be some duplication of goals, so the number is more likely to be around half of that.

Again, at each level, we just add more detail to describe how the prime objective will be achieved.

Let's take one of the departmental goals from the FurnFast sales department:

1.4.3.4 Engage followers by posting relevant content regularly

As we're getting closer to the detail of the tasks, we need to start thinking about specifying the detail of each task on the overall project plan.

Each task should be SMART – see the section on SMART.

Each task should also be defined in sufficient detail to allow it to be achieved to a defined timescale. The tasks should be unambiguous, and the output should be clearly defined and measurable.

So finally, by using the same brainstorming and thought process the managers and supervisors used to translate the management targets into departmental goals, the supervisors and workers will translate the departmental goals, into tasks, one element at a time:

In the FurnFast sales department, for example, the Social Media Coordinator and the Social Media Clerk agreed to:

1.4.3.4.1	Create a profile, on each of the chosen social media platforms, by [DATE]
1.4.3.4.2	Create a social media plan, to post to each platform, by [DATE]
1.4.3.4.3	Collate a portfolio of content and keep it updated, by [DATE]
1.4.3.4.4	Achieve 10k followers by [DATE]
1.4.3.4.5	And so on.

It is now possible to see that, for example, 'Creating a social media plan' is going to support the achievement of the Prime Objective.

We are using the cascade process to translate the Boardroom narrative into words that everyone can easily understand, and create a portfolio of tasks to deliver the required change.

In this straightforward example, we demonstrate the link between the Prime Objective and the tasks. We used the numbering system to allow us to track the individual tasks since they won't always be presented together in the format shown here. Some tasks appear to be similar; the numbering ensures they're not muddled.

At each tier of the cascade, the number of elements increased. In this example, we started with one objective, which became 19 top-level, at the worker level, there could be more than 1000 tasks, all clearly defined.

1 Prime Objective

19 top-level goals

105 management targets

260 departmental goals

1000+ operational tasks

By going to this level of detail, the objective can be cascaded into the organisation and turned into tasks for individuals.

The worker level tasks are a *to-do list*; they are tasks which can be used to define work schedules.

In reality, cascading is slightly more complicated than this exercise demonstrates. However, with a highly motivated management team, the cascading process shouldn't be a chore.

In this section, I've mentioned project plans several times. I'm not talking about complex plans; for me, a project plan has to be simple otherwise people won't be able to understand it.

Obviously, there are some good software packages that can support your project plan, but a good alternative is a simple table.

A simple project plan is like a route plan; it describes exactly what is going to happen, with timescales and responsibilities.

PROJECT PLAN					
Task Name	Start	End	Duration	Links	Responsibility
1.1.1.1.1.1 - Get a FaceBook account	4/4/2016	4/4/2016	1 day	-	Jamie
1.1.1.1.1.2 Build the FaceBook page	5/4/2016	7/4/2016	3 days	1.1.1.1.1.1	Jamie
1.1.1.1.1.3 Link the FaceBook page to the website	7/4/2016	7/4/2016	-	1.1.1.1.1.2	Jamie
1.1.1.1.1.4 Add a FaceBook link to marketing material	5/4/2016	2/5/2016	27 days	1.1.1.1.1.1	Sandra

Table Two: Tabulated Project Plan

Management

Poor implementation is considered to be the root cause of more failures than a poor Business Plan.

In reality, poor execution is a direct result of a poor plan. Therefore, failure during the implementation stage indicates there is a significant problem with the Business Plan.

The plan should carry enough detail to show everyone in the organisation who should be doing what, and when.

Organisations usually only have one attempt at this, so it's important to get it right from the outset. Management needs to provide insight, persuade, guide, convince, support, and reduce fear.

Management needs to tell everyone what the objective is – get personal, explaining how and why each individual is involved.

What I often see is the manager making a poor presentation or unconvincing statement (nervously) and then scampering back to their office.

It must be stressed, from the outset, the changes are not going to lead to job losses – it is essential for the change not to be seen as a workforce reduction exercise. Obviously, it's an excellent opportunity to look at costs, but don't let it be the prime driver.

The objective is not a manpower reduction exercise. Cost-cutting, if deemed necessary, is a secondary issue, maybe as a means of funding the changes.

Unless each manager comes across as strong, confident, and determined, individuals within the organisation will get nervous. If the workforce gets nervous, the objective will not be achieved, and individuals will start leaving for a more secure job.

Formulating the tasks

Formulating the tasks at the different levels of the organisation is the crucial part of the cascading process, it converts the objective into jobs which people can understand and can commit to completing.

It's essential that we involve the individuals responsible for doing the job – in other words, don't impose tasks upon anyone; because they won't understand it, they won't agree to it, and they simply won't do it.

The success of the cascading process relies on the leadership skills and expertise of individuals in each successive level of management.

Each task must be understood at every level; there should be a commitment to achieving what is required. Individuals should be motivated, feel proud to be an important part of a team, and be happy to contribute to the overall achievement of the objective.

Everyone in the organisation plays a vital role, and it's only after the collation of the tasks at every level that the size of the project can be appreciated.

At this stage, the links and dependencies can start to be made between elements of the project; at the same time, any visible gaps and conflicts can be highlighted.

Conflicting targets are a common occurrence; the reason for this is that initially, within the project, the managers are working independently of each other.

Each manager has great ideas, but those ideas can conflict.

For example, manufacturing managers may be looking to increase production output, and this requires them to reduce the stoppages – one way of doing this is by running the machines longer.

But the effect of this may conflict with the stock manager's plan to "Achieve 100% schedule adherence" because the schedule often only specifies what is required in stock and takes no account of the optimum manufacturing parameters.

In this, and similar cases, each manager needs to consider the possibility of achieving both targets. Otherwise, a compromise may need to be reached. Every conflict must be thoroughly discussed, and the solution has to be completely understood and recorded.

Simple management tools can be used to help make decisions, solve problems and formulate the tasks.

SMART objectives, targets and tasks

All objectives, targets and tasks should include critical metrics to make them SMART. I'm not going to go into the detail of SMART here; most managers are aware of SMART and what it means.

Specific   What exactly are we going to do?
Measurable   How are we going to measure the output?
Achievable   Can we do this?
Relevant   Will this task support the objective?
Time-based   When will this be completed?

The answer to the last question is that change never actually ends. What organisations find, as they're getting close to achieving the planned objective, is a growing momentum which creates a desire to do more – to set a new goal.

Organisations that undertake the process of change tend to get an appetite for more change – for greater improvement, more significant market share or more profitability. It is important to keep the momentum going.

That's it!

I hope you found the book useful. Remember, it's about the multi-stage development of plans – from the vision to the strategy, and then the cascading and communicating of those plans into the organisation, level-by-level.

I'm always interested in hearing any feedback; you can contact me through my publisher using the email address info@pen-2-paper.co.uk.

Review:
Section 4 put everything into practice:

- The directors must decide what's important to the organisation and what needs to be measured.

- The directors need to translate the vision into something which defines what the organisation aims to achieve – the Prime Objective.

- The cascade translates the prime objective into something which is understandable.

- The strategy meeting is critical to the realisation of the vision and the achievement of the Prime Objective. Expect a director-level strategy meeting to last for one full day. Aim for 100% attendance; all directors must give this meeting their full attention.

- We started with a vision. With the directors, we translated the vision into the Prime Objective. Then we fine-tuned the Prime Objective, added detail and converted it into the strategy. The next stage is for the directors to cascade the strategy down to the managers.

- Using the same brainstorming and thought process the directors used to translate the Prime Objective into the strategy, the directors and managers will translate the strategy into management targets, one element at a time.

- Again, using the same brainstorming and thought process the directors and managers used to translate the strategy into management targets, the managers and supervisors will translate the management targets into departmental goals, one element at a time.

- Finally, using the same brainstorming and thought process the managers and supervisors used to translate the management targets into departmental goals, the supervisors and workers will translate the departmental goals, into tasks, one element at a time.

- We used the cascade process to translate the Boardroom narrative into words that everyone can easily understand and use to deliver the planned changes.

ANNEX ONE

FURNFAST ORGANISATION

FurnFast Organisation Profile

Managing Director　　PA to MD

Financial Director　　Senior Mgt Accountant　　Accountants
　　　　　　　　　　　　Purchasing Officer　　　　Senior Buyer
　　　　　　　　　　　　Financial Accountant　　　Accounts
　　　　　　　　　　　　　　　　　　　　　　　　Collection
　　　　　　　　　　　　　　　　　　　　　　　　Salaries

Technical Director　　R&D Manager　　　　　　Designers
　　　　　　　　　　　　　　　　　　　　　　　　Engineer
　　　　　　　　　　　　　　　　　　　　　　　　Tester
　　　　　　　　　　　　Support Manager　　　　　Trainers
　　　　　　　　　　　　　　　　　　　　　　　　Engineer
　　　　　　　　　　　　　　　　　　　　　　　　Authors
　　　　　　　　　　　　　　　　　　　　　　　　Hotline

Sales Director　　　　Sales Manager　　　　　　Executives
　　　　　　　　　　　　　　　　　　　　　　　　Coordinator
　　　　　　　　　　　　　　　　　　　　　　　　Clerks
　　　　　　　　　　　　Marketing Manager　　　　Advertising
　　　　　　　　　　　　　　　　　　　　　　　　Writer
　　　　　　　　　　　　　　　　　　　　　　　　Print buyer
　　　　　　　　　　　　　　　　　　　　　　　　Coordinator
　　　　　　　　　　　　　　　　　　　　　　　　Artist
　　　　　　　　　　　　　　　　　　　　　　　　Webmaster
　　　　　　　　　　　　　　　　　　　　　　　　Social media
　　　　　　　　　　　　　　　　　　　　　　　　Clerk

Operations Director	Manufacturing Mgr	Supervisors
	Manufacturing Mgr	Supervisors
	Packaging Manager	Supervisors
	Facilities Manager	Security
		Canteen
		Engineers
		Cleaners
	ICT Manager	Engineers
		Engineers
	Compliance Manager	Quality
		H&S
	Engineering Manager	Tooling
		Toolmakers
		Buyer
		Setters
		Maintenance
Logistics Director	Scheduling Manager	Purchasing
		Production
		Deliveries
	Warehouse Manager	Stock
		Inspection
		Picking
	Logistics Manager	Drivers
HR Director	HR Manager	Training
		Issues
	Recruitment Manager	Hiring

ANNEX TWO

FURNFAST PRODUCTS

FurnFast Product Profile

The organisation sells:

1. Threaded fasteners–self-tapping
2. Threaded fasteners–cap screw
3. Hanger Bolts
4. Lock Nuts
5. Spring Nuts
6. T–Nuts
7. Locking Washers
8. Flat Washers
9. Levelling Guides
10. Levelling Guides
11. Tack Strips
12. Nail Trim
13. Trim Nails

The organisation buys:

1. Bar and Strip Stock
2. Plastic Compounds for injection-moulding
3. Metal insert for injection-moulded levelling guide foot
4. Threaded Nuts
5. Trim Nails
6. Boxes
7. Bags
8. Tape
9. Tubes
10. Tube end caps

The organisation subcontracts:

1   Locking Washers manufacturing
2   Nail Trim manufacturing
3   T–Nuts manufacturing

The organisation makes:

1   Threaded fasteners – self-tapping
2   Threaded fasteners – cap screws
3   Hanger Bolts
4   Spring nuts
5   Flat Washers
6   Levelling Guides
7   Tack Strips

ANNEX THREE

FURNFAST LOGISTICS

FurnFast Logistics Profile

BEFORE v AFTER

	NOW	2025
Sales revenue	£60.0m	£120.0m
Value of items subcontracted	£16.4m	£45.0m
Value of items manufactured	£41.7m	£60.0m
Value of items factored	£1.9m	£15.0m
Number of items sold	100m	182.2m
Number of items subcontracted	2m	5.1m
Number of items manufactured	22m	28.6m
Number of items factored	76m	148.5m
Average component price:	£0.600	£0.660

ANNEX FOUR

FURNFAST MANUFACTURING

FurnFast Manufacturing Profile

Threaded fasteners   Thread/Head forming
Deburring

Hanger Bolts   Thread/Head forming
Deburring

Spring nuts   Blanking
Deburring
Heat treatment

Flat Washers   Blanking
Deburring

Levelling Guides   Thread/Head forming
Deburring
Surface Treatment

     M-Foot   Blanking
Pressing
Deburring
Surface Treatment

     P-Foot   Injection-moulding
Pressing

Tack Strips   Blanking
Deburring
Heat treatment

ANNEX FIVE

FURNFAST OPERATIONS

FurnFast Operational Profile

Machinery and Equipment:

Screw thread & head forming machines

Blanking presses with stock in-feed device

Forming presses

Injection Moulding presses

Working Hours:

<u>Factory, Warehouse and Support</u>

Continental 4 shift, week about.

12 hours (7-7) for 4 days.

Set holiday of 25 days per year

<u>Office Staff</u>

8 hours (8:30–5:00) for 5 days.

Flexible holidays, except for bank holidays–32 days per year.

Stock Levels:

No make to order.

All product from stock.

Stock levels geared to last 30-month order trend.

Customers urged to manage their own stock levels.

Order Intake Level:

Incoming orders accepted and processed during office hours.

250 customers generate 840 orders per week, including many urgent orders for immediate dispatch.

GLOSSARY

Baseline

The baseline is the starting point, used for comparison to all future performance measures and trends. The organisation should measure, monitor, analyse and report progress relative to the baseline.

Brainstorm

The spontaneous group discussion to generate ideas and solve problems. It allows free-thinking and often generates seemingly wild ideas which can develop into something useful.

Business Plan

The document describing an organisation's objectives and the strategies and detailed plans for achieving them. An effective plan is one that is available and can be understood by everyone in the organisation.

Cascading

The processing of passing the strategies and plans from the top of the organisation to the bottom of the organisation, adding detail at each level. The cascading process translates the objectives into tasks and activities.

Cause and Effect Analysis

The process of determining the real or potential causes of an effect by brainstorming and analysing the crucial attributes; typically - people, product, plant, or process.

Competitor

An individual or organisation that operates in the same environment or market, and can or does affect, directly or indirectly, your operation, especially the provision of products and services to customers.

Customer

An individual or organisation which receives products or services from another.

Director

A member of the board of an organisation, charged with defining strategy and monitoring performance at the highest level.

Evolution

The gradual development of something, often without any inputs. Evolution is an unplanned change phase.

Failure Mode and Effects Analysis

Highly structured, systematic techniques for failure analysis. Developed by reliability engineers to study problems that might arise from malfunctions of products, software, materials, processes and systems.

Foundation

The lowest load-bearing element of a structure; typically at ground level. In an organisational structure, everything is built on the foundation – the workers.

Head

A person in charge of something; such as a director or leader.

Hierarchy

A system in which members of an organisation are structured according to their authority.

Management (The)

The people with a collective responsibility for managing an organisation.

Management Tools

If used appropriately, Management Tools can help define and execute the strategy, engage with customers and employees, and improve and monitor performance.

Manager

The person with the responsibility for controlling part of an organisation and its activities.

Measuring

The process of ascertaining the status of products, software, materials, processes and systems, so that changes can be made to correct an existing or predicted deviation.

Meeting

A formal scheduled assembly of people with a defined objective.

Objective

A particular outcome that is to be achieved, often within a specified timeframe and with the available resources.

Organisation

A group of people working together, often in a hierarchy.

Pareto Analysis

Ranking a range of items which have different levels of significance. The purpose is to separate the 'vital few' from the 'useful many'.

PESTLE

A strategic analysis tool useful for understanding markets, and organisational status, potential and direction.

Plan

A detailed framework for achieving something.

Prime Objective

The most important outcome that is to be achieved, often within a specified timeframe and with the available resources. The Prime Objective defines the organisation's purpose.

Process Mapping

A detailed process map allows organisations to assess the current processes and systems. Can be used to identify organisational improvements.

Revolution

A dramatic and wide-reaching change in culture, attitude, and performance.

Route Plan

A Route Plan details the directions and distances to move from one place to another.

Service Level Agreement

A contract between the provider of a service and a user of that service, specifying the level of service that will be provided.

Statistical Process Control

A method of monitoring a process and its output through the use of statistical parameters and control charts.

Strategy

A high-level plan to achieve the objectives, especially the Prime Objective.

Success

The accomplishment of an objective.

Supervisor

The person with the responsibility for overseeing part of an organisation and its activities.

Task

A piece of work to be completed to accomplish an objective.

Vision

A statement capturing an organisation's view of its future.

Worker

A person who works hard to complete tasks.

INDEX

Approval	**58**
Baseline	**8**, 42, **70-72**
Benefits	**6**
Brainstorm	**61**, 91
Business Plan	21, 27, **30**, **36-38**, 42, **43-44**, 48, 58, 96
Cascading	5, 8, 21, 27, 34, **35**, 45, 73-74, **89-96**
Celebration	8, **66**
Change	**ii**, 2-10, **14**, 17, 21-26, **37**, 52, 56-58, 64-67, 96
Communication	5, 18, 27, 55
Competitor	14-17, 56, 78
Confidential	33, **55**
Control	6, 9, 59
Cost	**21**, 53, 81-96
Customer	9, 18-20, 52, 56, 70, 81-90
Director	5, 26-27, 42-48, **70-84**, 89-91
Dissent	53
Enthusiasm	54, 58
Evolution	14-15, 58
Expenditure	**58**
Failure Mode & Effects Analysis	**62**
Financial	6, 59, **81**

Foundation	2-4
Head	2-3, 5-6, 23-26, 70-75
Hierarchy	3-4
HR	**84**
Implement	2, 4-5, 30-37, 96
Improvement	6, **52-56**,
Incentives	52-56
Logistics	**83, Annex 3**
Management	2, 7-8, **23-26**, 30-35, 52-56, 58, 61, 65-68, **89-97**
Management Tools	23-26, **61-64**
Manager	3-5, 23-25, 42, 47-48, 75-79, 89-97
Measuring	**7, 20**
Meetings	**59-61**, 65-66, 79
Mission	**42**
Monitoring	6-8, 37, 64-66
Objective	6-7, 18-26, 37-38, 42-43, **75-97**
Operations	6, 8, 14, 45, 48, 58-59, 73, **Annex 5**
Performance	6-9, 30-33, 56-58, 70-75
PESTLE	15-17, **45-47**, 79-89
Planning	6, **15-17**, **33-35**, **36-37**, 48
Prime Objective	**42, 72-95**
Profit	8, 21, 52-56, 75-89
Project	6-8, 17-18, 56, **58-59**, **64-66**, 79-96
Recruitment	**61**
Responsibility	9, 38, 79, 89-95
Revenue	5, 21, 42, 70, 65-89

Revolution	14-15, 48, **56-58**, 72-75
Route Plan	17, 27, 37, **38-41**, 70, 94
Schedule	6, 64, 94
Sequence	6, 42
Service Level Agreements	**63**
Strategy	**79**
Structure	2-3, 5, 7, 26, **35-36**, 48-50, 64-65, 89
Success	2-3, 7-8, **20-21**, 95-96
Supervisor	3-5, 38, 42, 49, 53, 78-79, 89-95
Target	3, 6-7, 30-35, 42-45, 65, **97**
Task	17, 27, 34, **95-97**
Technical	42, 82
Technology	43-48
Time	31, 34, 42, 53, 73, 79
Training	23, 52, 59, 62, 66
Vision	7, 21, 23, **42**, 72-75, 79, 89, 98
Worker	3-6, 18-20, 23-33, 42-45, 53, 75-89